# CORE ENGLISH

# Out of
# This World

# CORE ENGLISH

# Out of This World

Ronald Caie, Hellen Matthews,
Anne Rigg and Anne Mitchell

SERIES EDITOR:
Colin Lamont

HEINEMANN EDUCATIONAL BOOKS

Heinemann Educational Books Ltd
Halley Court, Jordan Hill, Oxford OX2 8EJ

OXFORD LONDON EDINBURGH
MELBOURNE SYDNEY AUCKLAND
SINGAPORE MADRID ATHENS
IBADAN NAIROBI GABORONE HARARE
KINGSTON PORTSMOUTH (NH)

Core English
  Out of this world
  1. English literature—20th century
  I. Lamont, Colin   II. Mitchell, Anne
  820.8'00912     PR1148

  ISBN 0-435-10581-7

First published 1985
Reprinted 1985, 1987, 1988

Designed and typeset by Leaper and Gard Ltd, Bristol
Printed and bound in Great Britain by
Richard Clay Ltd, Bungay, Suffolk

# CONTENTS

# Acknowledgements

The authors and publishers wish to thank the following for permission to reproduce copyright material. It has not been possible to contact all copyright holders, and the publishers would be glad to hear from any unacknowledged copyright holders.

David Higham Associates and Ronald Duncan for *Man*, Part IV, Canto 3; Ronald Caie for 'You Fly the Shuttle', 'Unlucky Apollo 13', 'Death of an Astronaut', 'Alien Contact' and 'The Time of His Life'; Neil Davies for 'An Astronaut Spacewalking' from *Young Writers 23rd Year*, published by W.H. Smith; Bryn Griffiths for 'Bleep'; A D Peters & Co Ltd and Ray Bradbury for *Dark They Were and Golden Eyed* (adapted); 'The Gift' from *A Medicine for Melancholy*; 'Kaleidoscope' from *The Illustrated Man*; 'The Smile' from *The Day It Rained Forever*; and 'There Will Come Soft Rains'; Westminster Music Limited and David Bowie for 'A Space Oddity'; Carcanet Press Ltd and Edwin Morgan for 'Off-Course' and 'First Men on Mercury' from *Edwin Morgan: Poems of Thirty Years* (Carcanet, Manchester, 1982); Iain Crichton Smith for 'The Planets'; James Kirkup for 'Poem Written After Sighting an Unidentified Flying Object' from *Black Shadows, White Shadows: Poems of Peace and War* (Dent, 1971); The adaptation of 'The Fly' by Arthur Porges is reprinted by permission of the author and the author's agents, Scott Meredith Literary Agency Inc., 845 Third Avenue, New York, New York 10022; David Higham Associates Ltd for extract from *Chocky* by John Wyndham, which is reprinted by permission of the John Wyndham Estate; extract from *Grinny* by Nicholas Fisk is reprinted by permission of William Heinemann Limited; Harvey Unna & Stephen Durbridge Ltd and R C Scriven for 'The Marrog'; Random House Inc. and Edmond Hamilton for 'The Exile' from *The Best of Edmond Hamilton* (ed. Leigh Brackett Hamilton); A D Peters & Co Ltd and Roger McGough for 'Icarus Allsorts' and 'At Lunchtime' from *Modern Poets 10*; the poem 'Noah's Ark' from *Waving at Trains* and 'The Future' from *In the Glassroom*; Anthony Sheil Associates Ltd and Robert Sheckley for extract from *The Store of the Worlds* © Robert Sheckley, 1980; 'Harrison Bergeron' excerpted from *Welcome to the Monkey House* by Kurt Vonnegut Jr. Copyright © 1961 by Kurt Vonnegut Jr. Originally published in *Fantasy and Science Fiction*. Reprinted by permission of Delacorte Press/Seymour Lawrence; 'Examination Day' by Henry Slesar originally appeared in *Playboy* magazine: Copyright © 1958 by Playboy; The Guardian and Ian Ridpath for 'Journey into Space'; 'Saturn' words and music by Stevie Wonder and Michael Sembello © 1976 Jobete Music Co Inc and Black Bull Music Inc. All rights reserved. Used by permission of Jobete Music (Ltd.)/Black Bull Music. International copyright secured.

# 1

# **Space Travellers**

There was a witch, hump-backed and hooded,
Lived by herself in a burnt-out tree.
When storm winds shrieked and the moon was buried
And the dark of the forest was black as black,
She rose in the air like a rocket at sea,
    Riding the wind,
    Riding the night,
Riding the tempest to the moon and back.

There may be a man with a hump of silver,
Telescope eyes and a telephone ear,
Dials to twist and knobs to twiddle,
Waiting for a night when the skies are clear,
To shoot from the scaffold with a blazing track,
    Riding the dark,
    Riding the cold,
Riding the silence to the moon and back.

*James Nimmo*

# Man (Part IV, Canto 3)

It's not easy for me to tell you my feelings on that occasion.
I'm a man who was never troubled with any emotions
Particularly deep, as you might say.
That's why they selected me, I suppose.
They didn't want a neurotic, complicated guy,
Whose imagination might upset their calculations;
But somebody physically fit, technically able,
And in control.
Let me put it this way: my nervous system
was unlikely to short-circuit;
They didn't want a guy like you
Who might see some internal vision up there,
then forget to fire the retro-rocket: no offence of course . . .
The psycho-boys screened me for hours:
They said my normality was almost abnormal.
I suppose what they were looking for was somebody
whose emotional attachments were sufficient
to give him the will to live,
but insufficient to cause him to do anything foolish.
Yes, as you say, somebody who was unlikely to over
                    compensate
with an emotional gesture, commit hari-kari,
copulate with the universe or indulge in self-crucifixion,
whatever that is.
And as you suppose, they enquired pretty deeply into my
                    private life:
asked me about my feelings for my mother, my wife and kids
and whether I had any attachment to anybody, on the side.
They seemed pretty satisfied that none of this
Had fouled me up.
And of course, they asked me about my dreams.
I found this pretty embarrassing,
And they seemed pleased that I was embarrassed.
You see, they didn't want a guy
That was introspective or as complicated as a computer in
                    himself
   And certainly nobody who had any spiritual dilemmas.
I must say I got a clean sheet there.

There were questions I'd never considered
  so there were no problems you might say.
They asked me what I believed in and eventually
  I came up with: evolution and efficiency.
Yes. You find that hard to believe? That's how I am.
  Lift-off itself provided no new sensations,
We had gone through the drill too often
  and simulated every detail:
I found it hard to realize this was the real thing.
I remember noticing that the shape of the capsule
      reminded me of something but I couldn't think what,
Until I was strapped in, waiting for the count down,
  And, at the instant of blast off, I realized what it was:
      the exterior of the capsule was the shape of a cathode ray
        tube
And this, I suppose, made me wonder what the inside was
        like
  The first image was an easter egg.
And then a line of poetry came into my mind —
  God knows from where:
'Like a worm in the bud'. I nearly said it aloud.
That would have surprised them . . .
  But that was it. There was not time for any other thoughts.
Alone up there you're about as alone
  as a telephone operator
With the whole world talking to you;
  They even know your pulse rate,
And when you ought to make water.
  Sure.
And being in orbit gave me no new sensations either.
  You see, we'd been through it all before,
Down here in that gadget
  Which even has a revolving globe outside the porthole.
And of course you get no sense of speed,
  less than on a subway.
You are static, suspended, watching the earth turn round
  like an old cart wheel.
And you're kept busy, very:
      recording, checking, talking back
  to a computer, programming your position,
And fuel consumption: so busy, that sleep
  is the one compelling need up there;
Sleep, where your dreams alone are heavy.
Weightlessness is a wag: Puck, as you might say,

always up to some joke or tease
taking you unawares. Like when I coughed
    And moved into my own spit getting an eyeful,
getting my own back . . . or the crumbs
which refuse to drop.
But there was nothing new up there,
    leastways not till I opened the hatch
and took that brief walk with my rocket gun . . .
    It's something I didn't tell them,
Something I kept to myself,
        it had no scientific significance
Maybe even you will laugh at me
No, it wasn't fear. I would have told them that;
    But it wasn't fear, I had nothing to fear:
The capsule only forty feet away:
    My oxygen line, straight and not fouled up;
And below me: the earth turning so gently
    trailing its shawl of clouds;
And as I watched it, I felt an emotion so strong
    the tears spurted from my eyes.
It wasn't homesickness, but earthsickness;
    A yearning, like a tide inside of me;
I would have swopped the whole universe
    for any foothold on that ball of dirt
Which I wanted then, and loved
    more than I've ever wanted or loved a woman;
I desired the earth, not any part nor any person,
    But it, where I belonged: the whole was home to me.
I guess I was the first man –
    for you can't count Him as one, I suppose? –
to feel such tenderness for the whole damn place
    and any bastard on it.
No, I don't feel it any more. Well, not so intensely.
    Maybe you have to be cut off to be in contact?
Or, maybe, it's only when the body has no weight
    that love becomes the one imponderable?
But, as I say, I didn't tell them about it.

*Ronald Duncan*

4

# 3

# Journey into Space

You are strapped to a couch in the nose of the space shuttle, 200ft above the swamplands of Cape Canaveral. Gone are the days of cumbersome spacesuits, for flying on the Shuttle is more like flying on a high-performance jet plane than on a spacecraft.

You are kitted out in light-blue jacket and trousers made of flameproof material, but you wear a helmet in case the Shuttle springs a leak during its ascent.

On the flight deck above you, the NASA astro-pilots are running down the last entries in their checklist. You are tucked out of their way on the mid-deck below.

A call comes over the intercom from mission control: 'Go for main engine start.' It is seven seconds to lift-off. You hear three rapid bangs as the main engines ignite, gulping liquid hydrogen and liquid oxygen fuel at the rate of one thousand gallons a second.

As the engines build up thrust, you feel the 'twang': the whole vehicle tilts slightly, gently rocking you forward about 20 inches in your seat. Then it settles back again. Now the solid-fuelled boosters at the Shuttle's sides ignite with two loud explosions, finally prising you away from the Earth.

The Shuttle rises like a highspeed lift into the blue Florida sky. You are off on your first trip into space. Out of the side window you see the launch tower slipping past. Then the whole world appears to spin round as the Shuttle rolls through 120 degrees to set it on the right course out over the Atlantic.

There is no sensation of speed until the Shuttle punches through a low deck of cloud.

As the Shuttle accelerates it feels as though a heavy hand is pressing you down into your seat. Your arms and legs feel twice as heavy as they do on Earth.

Less than a minute after lift-off you feel the main engines throttle back to prevent the acceleration forces from becoming too great as the Shuttle goes supersonic. Once you are past the speed of sound, the ride becomes much smoother and quieter. Outside the window, the sky has turned black.

Two minutes into the flight a slight deceleration tells you that the solid rockets are nearing the end of their fuel. For half a second the side window is filled by a bright orange flame as the solid rockets are fired off. Out of the window you see them fall away. Already, you are 30 miles high.

Now the ride becomes so smooth that if you closed your eyes you would hardly know you were moving, were it not for the steadily increasing g-forces. The Shuttle is racing upwards at 3,000 miles per hour. Over the headset from mission control comes a brief call to confirm that the Shuttle is heading safely for orbit.

Eight and a half minutes into the flight, the half million gallons of fuel in the external tank is exhausted and the main engines cut off. Now you start to experience weightlessness.

At first it feels as though you are hanging upside down. You float upwards in your seat, and you feel the blood rushing to your head, making your face puffy and your nose stuffy. Nasal congestion will probably remain with you throughout the flight, and may give you a headache during the first day in space.

While you are coming to terms with these strange sensations, the external fuel tank is jettisoned to fall back into the atmosphere and burn up. Next, the orbital manoeuvring system engines fire to push the Shuttle into orbit.

It has been 12 minutes since lift-off, and you have travelled little more than 150 miles upwards, yet it has been the most exciting journey of your life. Gently you unstrap yourself and for the first time get the full feeling of weightlessness. Instinctively you reach out to grab hold of something to steady yourself, but you are floating without falling.

Freed of the downward pull of gravity, your arms and shoulders hunch up, your knees bend and your arms float out in front of you. When trying to move about, you first of all push off too hard and find yourself running into the opposite wall. But soon you learn to coordinate your movements in weightlessness.

You float through the hatch to the upper deck to watch the astronauts at work. Looking at them you see their puffy faces, hear their nasal voices and notice their legs getting skinny, like crow's legs, as the blood moves into the upper parts of their bodies.

You must be careful not to move your head around too much during the first day or so in orbit, for that produces feelings of space sickness.

Through the panoramic windows on the flight deck you can begin to appreciate the beauty of the Earth below: clouds like layers of whipped cream overlying rich blue-green oceans, the patchwork pattern of fields, the lace embroidery of snow-topped mountains, the wash-board-like effect of sand dunes, and a plume of smoke from an active volcano.

If you look carefully, you can even see roads and railways and the wake of ships at sea.

When sunset comes, as it does every 90 minutes, it forms a spectacular rainbow band of colours along the curving horizon.

Soon it is time for dinner – if space sickness has not dulled your appetite. To make yourself useful, you are assigned to be cook for tonight. Evening meal consists of shrimp cocktail, steak with rice and broccoli, fruit cocktail, and butterscotch pudding, washed down with a grape drink.

Some space food is dehydrated, some comes in cans and some is in pouches that need heating. The shuttle's galley on the mid-deck is equipped with an electric oven and hot and cold water dispensers.

You inject water into the shrimp, rice and broccoli, place the steak in the oven, and arrange the completed items on the food trays. Those astronauts who are not feeling too queasy join you around the tables. Drinks are squeezed from concertina-like bottles, but most foods are eaten from cans or plastic pouches with a spoon and fork.

Washing facilities consist of a small enclosed sink through which water is drawn by an airflow. You turn it on, adjust the water temperature, squirt some soap into your palm, and wash your hands. To wash other parts of your body you use a damp washcloth. You clean your teeth with edible toothpaste.

Proper beds are unnecessary in weightlessness. Instead, you sleep zipped up in a sleeping bag attached to the wall of the mid-deck. On your first night in space you will probably be too excited to go to bed at first, but when you do so you will find that sleeping in weightlessness is comfortable and deeply relaxing.

After five days in space, your adventure is coming to a close. Reluctantly you strap yourself into your seat in preparation for re-entry into the Earth's atmosphere.

Above Australia, the commander turns the Shuttle so that it is travelling tail first. A slight push tells you that the orbital manoeuvring system engines have fired to slow the Shuttle for its drop back to Earth. In an hour's time you will be on the ground.

The commander pitches the Shuttle so that its insulated underside takes the heat of re-entry. Above the Pacific Ocean, 60 miles up and travelling at 25 times the speed of sound, you hit the upper edge of the atmosphere.

Friction with the air creates a reddish-pink glow around the Shuttle, turning orange near the nose where temperatures are hottest. It seems as though you are flying through a neon tube.

In spite of the high speed of re-entry, the Shuttle flies smoothly. As the Shuttle slows, you feel as though you are being crushed by a great weight – after a week spent weightless, you have forgotten what gravity feels like.

About half-an-hour after the start of re-entry, the Shuttle is plunging in a steep glide towards the landing strip at Cape Canaveral, next to the launch pad from which you departed.

The Shuttle goes subsonic only four minutes before touchdown. Fourteen seconds after the wheels come down, the Shuttle lands on the runway at 215 mph, fifty per cent faster than a commercial jet. It rolls for a further two miles before coming to a halt.

You feel relieved, and perhaps a little queasy, after the high-speed descent. Rather unsteadily, you descend the steps to a waiting bus, possibly eager to repeat the experience one day, or perhaps having decided never to leave the Earth again.

*Ian Ridpath*

# An Astronaut Spacewalking

He floats, tap-dancing on infinity,
  Looking like an obese statue;
His round, marble head
  Dark and faceless.

He drifts, like a log on water,
  Connected to existence by a mere thread;
Come cosmic ray or meteor
  He still walks on nothing

Then he returns to his capsule,
  Back to the little world in which he lives
Out of the vacuum
  Back to reality.

*Neil Davies*

# 5

# Unlucky Apollo 13

## or...
## 'Hey, We've Got a Problem Here!'

The three astronauts, Jim Lovell, Jack Swigert and Fred Haise, could now relax. They had just completed a successful telecast to Earth and it was time for their rest period.

It was to be the third Moon landing. Their spacecraft *Odyssey* with its moonlander *Aquarius* was outward bound and all systems looked good. For two days they had coasted silently towards their target and already the people back on Earth were beginning to forget them. Space journeys had been made before, they were becoming routine, and space journeys that did not go wrong did not make exciting reading in the newspapers.

There had been some interest at the beginning of the flight because of the mission's number — *Apollo 13* — and one or two astrologers had shaken their heads doubtfully. This didn't worry the spaceflight Commander's wife, Marilyn Lovell. She told reporters that she was not at all concerned by the number and when told that the rocket had lifted off at 13.13 hours and that the most critical part of the mission was to take place near the Moon on April 13th she laughed and said it was all pure coincidence. She had no superstitions.

But the flight had not been without its setbacks. When the great Saturn rocket soared up from the launching pad on a tower of flame there had been a few anxious moments. One of the five motors on the second stage had shut down before it was supposed to and it had been touch and go as to whether the three man crew would ever get into Earth orbit let alone make the 477,714 miles' journey to the Moon and back. Later, with typical understatement, Mission Control had described it rather flatly as 'a less-than-perfect launch'.

When April 13th dawned on Earth, the spacecraft was within a few thousand miles of the Moon. Earth seemed small in the distance and through the ports of the command module the crew marvelled at the approaching moonscape. Already they could see mountains and plains, enormous craters and the beautiful Sea of Tranquility where nine

months earlier Neil Armstrong had landed the tiny *Eagle* spacecraft and so become the first man to set foot upon the surface of another world. Somewhere down there the Stars and Stripes still flew, supported in the vacuum of space by stiffening wires.

It was 9 p.m. at the Mission Control Centre in Houston when they called to congratulate the astronauts on their successful TV transmission which had been viewed by hundreds of millions of people on Earth. Suddenly Jack Swigert interrupted with the words, 'Hey, we've got a problem here!' There had been what he coolly described as 'a pretty large bang'.

Within minutes the oxygen readings in the *Odyssey* spacecraft plunged to zero, one of the three vital electrical systems failed and the crew reported seeing clouds of gas leaking off into space. In fact, one of the oxygen tanks in the service module had exploded, ripping a huge hole in the side of the spacecraft.

For the next eighty minutes there was a continuous technical exchange between Mission Control at Houston and the stricken spacecraft. Then the order came, 'Abandon the command module *Odyssey* and board the moonlander, *Aquarius*. And so, with only fifteen minutes of life-support left the three astronauts crawled through the connecting tunnel into the two man *Aquarius*. They closed and sealed the hatches behind them and prepared for the long, cold return journey to Earth in the moonlander. For the next three days they lived with the threat of death hanging over them. Only when they returned to Earth orbit would they be able to tell whether the damage to the service module was slight enough to enable them to make a safe landing on Earth. There were two alternatives — being burned alive in the capsule as they hurtled out of control through the upper atmosphere or, more likely, missing Earth altogether and drifting on in space until all their oxygen ran out and they died of asphyxiation.

It is now many years since that heroic journey through a quarter million miles of space and the story has already become history. Miraculously all went well for unlucky *Apollo 13* and a safe landing was made.

Today all three astronauts are alive and well. Jim Lovell, the commander, eventually retired from the space business and now works for a towing company in Houston. But the other two, Fred Haise and Jack Swigert, are still astronauts and in 1977 Fred Haise became one of the first men to pilot the new Space Shuttle in high altitude tests.

Just for the Record . . .

The *Apollo 13* crew may not have landed on the Moon, but there was one compensation. They go down on record as having travelled further from the planet Earth than anyone.

At 1.21 a.m. British Standard Time on 15th April 1970 they were 158 miles above the lunar surface on the far side. That was 248,655 miles above the surface of the Earth. To date, no one has ever been further away from home.

*Ronald Caie*

# 6

# Bleep

*Bleep!* said the little robot spacecraft,
squatting infinitely alone
in the blinding dust of Venus,
*bleep . . . bleep . . . bleep* – Bleep
Fifty-million miles of empty space
were crossed in seconds –
mankind knew of contact
with the sky's love goddess at last –
and earphones jabbered at Jodrell Bank.

But nothing could be made there
of such strange noises
(for the bleeps were in Russian, you see);
only the Russian scientists, somewhere in
Siberia,
knew what such noises meant . . .

And the bleeps said: 'By God! By Comrade
Khrushchev –
it's bloody hot here! It's far too hot
for a little Russian rocket like me – I'm
getting out of here!'

'Nonsense,' replied the scientists,
somewhere in Siberia, 'you can't *feel*
anything, you're only a robot,
and you just can't get out, so there!'
(But, secretly, they worried about
radiation and mutation,
computerized constipation,
and galactic goo gumming up the works.)

'Like hell I can't get out,'
snarled the little rocket,
'just you watch my space-dust!'
and he took off for Alpha Centauri
at a most remarkable speed.

'Amazing!' cried the scientists,
as the dot on the telescope dwindled
out into the dark infinity.

*Bleep*, said the little spacecraft,
nipping smartly past Neptune,
*bleep . . . bleep . . . bleep . . . bleep . . .*

*Bryn Griffiths*

# 7

# The Gift

Tomorrow would be Christmas and even while the three of them rode to the rocket port, the mother and father were worried. It was the boy's first flight into space, his very first time in a rocket, and they wanted everything to be perfect. So when, at the customs table, they were forced to leave behind his gift which exceeded the weight limit by no more than a few ounces and the little tree with the lovely white candles, they felt themselves deprived of the season and their love.

The boy was waiting for them in the Terminal room. Walking towards him, after their unsuccessful clash with the Interplanetary officials, the mother and father whispered to each other.

'What shall we do?'

'Nothing, nothing. What *can* we do?

'Silly rules!'

'And he so wanted the tree!'

The siren gave a great howl and people pressed forward into the Mars Rocket. The mother and father walked at the very last, their small pale son between them, silent.

'I'll think of something,' said the father.

'What . . . ?' asked the boy.

And the rocket took off and they were flung headlong into dark space.

The rocket moved and left fire behind and left Earth behind on which the date was 24 December, 2052, heading out into a place where there was no time at all, no month, no year, no hour. They slept away the rest of the first 'day'. Near midnight, by their Earth-time New York watches, the boy awoke and said, 'I want to go and look out of the porthole.'

There was only one port, a 'window' of immensely thick glass, of some size, up on the next deck.

'Not quite yet,' said the father. 'I'll take you up later.'

'I want to see where we are and where we're going.'

'I want you to wait, for a reason,' said the father.

He had been lying awake, turning this way and that, thinking of the abandoned gift, the problem of the season, the lost tree and the white candles. And at last, sitting up, no more than five minutes ago, he believed he had found a plan. He need only carry it out and this journey would be fine and joyous indeed.

'Son,' he said, 'in exactly one half-hour it will be Christmas.'

'Oh,' said the mother, dismayed that he had mentioned it. Somehow she had rather hoped the boy would forget.

The boy's face grew feverish and his lips trembled. 'I know, I know. Will I get a present, will I? Will I have a tree? You promised –'

'Yes, yes, all that, and more,' said the father.

The mother started. 'But –'

'I mean it,' said the father. 'I really mean it. All and more, much more. Excuse me, now. I'll be back.'

He left them for about twenty minutes. When he came back he was smiling. 'Almost time.'

'Can I hold your watch?' asked the boy, and the watch was handed over and he held it ticking in his fingers as the rest of the hour drifted by in fire and silence and unfelt motion.

'It's Christmas *now*! Christmas! Where's my present?'

'Here we go,' said the father, and took his boy by the shoulder and led him from the room, down the hall, up a ramp-way, his wife following.

'I don't understand,' she kept saying.

'You will. Here we are,' said the father.

They had stopped at the closed door of a large cabin. The father tapped three times and then twice, in a code. The door opened and the light in the cabin went out and there was a whisper of voices.

'Go on in, son,' said the father.

'It's dark.'

'I'll hold your hand. Come on, mama.'

They stepped into the room and the door shut, and the room was very dark indeed. And before them loomed a great glass eye, the porthole, a window four feet high and six feet wide, from which they could look out into space.

The boy gasped.

Behind him, the father and the mother gasped with him, and then in the dark room some people began to sing.

'Merry Christmas, son,' said the father.

And the voices in the room sang the old, the familiar carols, and the boy moved forward slowly until his face was pressed against the cool glass of the port. And he stood there for a long long time, just looking and looking out into space and the deep night at the burning and the burning of ten billion billion white and lovely candles. . . .

*Ray Bradbury*

# 8

# A Space Oddity

Ground Control to Major Tom . . .
Ground Control to Major Tom . . .
Take your protein pills
And put your helmet on.
Ground Control to Major Tom . . .
Commencing countdown . . . engines on . . .
Check ignition and may God's love be with you.

This is Ground Control to Major Tom
You've really made the grade
And the papers want to know whose shirts you wear . . .
Now it's time to leave the capsule, if you dare.

This is Major Tom to Ground Control.
I'm stepping through the door,
And I'm floating in a most peculiar way,
And the stars are very different today,
For here am I sitting in my tin can
Far above the world,
The Planet Earth is blue
And there's nothing I can do.
Though I'm past one hundred thousand miles
I'm feeling very still,
And I think my spaceship knows which way to go.
Tell my wife I love her very much, she knows . . .

Ground Control to Major Tom . . .
Your circuit's dead . . . there's something wrong . . .
Can you hear me Major Tom?
Can you hear me Major Tom?
Can you hear me Major Tom?
Can you . . .

Here am I floating
Far above the Moon,
The Planet Earth is blue
And there's nothing I can do.

*David Bowie*

17

# 9

# Death of an Astronaut

When the explosion came, it came suddenly
Captain Stark felt it rather than heard it,
A rumbling shock reverberating in the bones.
Then the alarms, the buzzers and the klaxons
And the instrument panel lit up
Like a Christmas tree
A million miles from Bethlehem.

Next, a voice from Earth,
The inevitable Mission Control –
'*Athena One*, you have a major malfunction.
Telemetry indicates total decompression imminent.
Please don your helmets and pressurise your suits.'

A short calm glance to Major Anderson
Across the consul.
No words. Eyes told all.
Then the helmets on and things to do –
And –
The last loud bang ripped across the craft
And sent the Captain spinning into space
With nuts and bolts and bits of foil
And the hopes of a million men on Earth.
Dear God in Heaven!
What a way to go!

'Captain Stark?
Mission Control.
Major malfunction.
Your wife?
Yes.
Anything we can do?
Two hours of oxygen only.
No call from Major Anderson.'

His silent suit goes sparkling in the sun
A little blood space-frozen at the punctures.

'Dear Mary
What can I say? So near
And yet a million miles away.
Tell little John I love him –
Must go now
The stars and suns are fading at my brow.'

*Ronald Caie*

# 10

# Kaleidoscope

The first concussion cut the rocket up the side with a giant can opener. The men were thrown out into space like a dozen wriggling silverfish. They were scattered into a dark sea; and the ship, in a million pieces, went on, a meteor swarm seeking a lost sun.

'Barkley, Barkley, where are you?'

The sound of voices calling like children on a cold night.

'Woode, Woode!'

'Captain!'

'Hollis, Hollis, this is Stone.'

'Stone, this is Hollis. Where are you?'

'I don't know. How can I? Which way is up? I'm falling. Good God, I'm falling.'

They fell as pebbles fall down wells. They were scattered from a gigantic throw. And now instead of men there were only voices – all kinds of voices, disembodied and impassioned, in varying degrees of terror and resignation.

'We're going away from each other.'

This was true. Hollis, swinging head over heels, knew this was true. He knew it with a vague acceptance. They were parting to go their separate ways, and nothing could bring them back. They were wearing their sealed-tight space suits with the glass tubes over their pale faces, but they hadn't had time to lock on their force units. With them they could be small lifeboats in space, saving themselves, saving others, collecting together, finding each other until they were an island of men with some plan. But without the force units snapped to their shoulders they were meteors, senseless, each going to a separate and irrevocable fate.

A period of perhaps ten minutes elapsed while the first terror died and a metallic calm took its place. Space began to weave its strange voices in and out, on a great dark loom, crossing, re-crossing, making a final pattern.

'Stone to Hollis. How long can we talk by phone?'

'It depends on how fast you're going your way and I'm going mine.'

'An hour, I make it.'

'That should do it,' said Hollis, abstracted and quiet.

'What happened?' asked Hollis a minute later.

'The rocket blew up, that's all. Rockets do blow up.'

'Which way are you going?'

'It looks like I'll hit the Moon.'

'It's Earth for me. Back to old Mother Earth at ten thousand miles per hour. I'll burn like a match.' Hollis thought of it with a queer abstraction of mind. He seemed to be removed from his body, watching it fall down and down through space, as objective as he had been in regard to the first falling snowflakes of a winter season long gone.

The others were silent, thinking of the destiny that had brought them to this, falling, falling, and nothing they could do to change it. Even the Captain was quiet, for there was no command or plan he knew that could put things back together again.

\*     \*     \*

I'll burn, he thought, and be scattered in ashes all over the continental lands. I'll be put to use. Just a little bit, but ashes are ashes and they'll add to the land.

He fell swiftly, like a bullet, like a pebble, like an iron weight, objective, objective all of the time now, not sad or happy or anything, but only wishing he could do a good thing now that everything was gone, a good thing for just himself to know about.

When I hit the atmosphere, I'll burn like a meteor.

'I wonder,' he said, 'if anyone'll see me?'

The small boy on the country road looked up and screamed. 'Look, Mom, look! A falling star!'

The blazing white star fell down the sky of dusk in Illinois.

'Make a wish,' said his mother. 'Make a wish.'

*Ray Bradbury*

21

# Off Course

the golden flood     the weightless seat
the cabin song     the pitch black
the growing beard     the floating crumb
the shining rendezvous     the orbit wisecrack
the hot spacesuit     the smuggled mouth-organ
the imaginary somersault     the visionary sunrise
the turning continents     the space debris
the golden lifeline     the space walk
the crawling deltas     the camera moon
the pitch velvet     the rough sleep
the crackling headphone     the space silence
the turning earth     the lifeline continents
the cabin sunrise     the hot flood
the shining spacesuit     the growing moon
   the crackling somersault     the smuggled orbit
   the rough moon     the visionary rendezvous
   the weightless headphone     the cabin debris
   the floating lifeline     the pitch sleep
   the crawling camera     the turning silence
   the space crumb     the crackling beard
   the orbit mouth-organ     the floating song

*Edwin Morgan*

# The Planets

All the planets have been named
after the gods, but one at birth
seemed so shy and so ashamed
they simply called it Earth.

But there's this difference between
these godlike planets and our own
though they shine with lovely sheen
they are lifeless lands of stone.

*Iain Crichton Smith*

# Poem Written After Sighting an Unidentified Flying Object

They are above us,
Beyond us and around us,
Out of space out of time

Between star and star,
New moons, and beings wiser
Than ourselves, approach.

Our earth is rotten
As a fruit about to drop
Into nothingness.

They are gardeners
Of space, who come to tend us.
Strangers, they love us.

In ages long past
They came to our planet.
We drove them away.

Ever since that day
Our world moves to destruction.
Death grows among us.

Only if we call
To the beautiful strangers
Will our peace return.

I know they watch me
As I write this poem now.
Poets are cosmic.

I feel their silence
Like words, their absence like love.
We must turn to them.

We must watch for them.
We must give our hearts and souls,
Open eyes and arms

Look to the heavens
And upon the ground for signs.
They are among us.

And we shall see them
With the eyes of vision, if
We have sense to see.

And we shall know them
By their purity and grace,
If we have hearts to feel.

They are above us,
Beyond us and around us,
Out of space out of time.

*James Kirkup*

# 14

# Dark They Were and Golden-Eyed

The rocket cooled in the meadow winds. From it stepped a man, a woman and three children. The other passengers whispered away across the Martian meadow, leaving the man alone among his family.

He felt his hair flutter and his body tense. His wife seemed almost to whirl away in smoke. The children might at any moment be blown away like seeds. They looked up at him. His face was cold.

'What's wrong?' asked his wife.

'Let's go back on the rocket.'

'Go back to Earth?'

'Yes! Listen!'

The wind blew as if at any instant it would draw his soul from him. He felt as if he would dissolve and his past would be burned away.

They looked at the Martian hills, worn with the years. The old cities lay like children's delicate bones among the blowing lakes of grass.

'Chin up, Harry,' said his wife. 'It's too late. We've come over sixty-million miles'.

The yellow-haired children shouted at the deep dome of the Martian sky. There was no answer but the racing hiss of wind through the stiff grass.

He picked up the luggage in his cold hands. 'Here we go,' he said – a man standing on the edge of a sea, ready to wade in and be drowned.

They walked into town.

Their name was Bittering. Harry and his wife Cora; Dan, Laura and David. They built a small white cottage but the fear was never gone.

'I feel like a salt crystal,' he said, 'in a mountain stream being washed away. We don't belong here. This is Mars. It was meant for Martians. For Heaven's sake, Cora, let's buy tickets for home.'

But she only shook her head. 'One day the atom bombs will fix Earth. Then we'll be safe here.'

Something made him check everything each morning –

precisely as if he expected something to be wrong. But he forced himself to be cheerful.

'Colonial days all over again,' he declared. 'Why, in ten years there'll be a million Earth Men on Mars. They said we'd fail. Said the Martians would resent our invasion. But did we find Martians? Not a living soul, just their empty cities. Right?'

A river of wind submerged the house, rattling the windows.

'Maybe there are Martians and we don't see,' said David. 'Sometimes I think I hear them at nights. I hear the wind, the sand hits my window. I get scared. I think I see things moving in the towns in the mountains. And I wonder if those Martians mind us living here and will do something to us for coming.'

'Nonsense,' Mr Bittering replied. 'All dead cities have ghosts. Your imagination makes ghosts in your mind.'

'Just the same,' said David, 'I bet something happens.'

Something happened that afternoon.

The radio flash announced the war. Atom bombs had hit New York. All the space rockets blown up. They were stranded on Mars. A thousand of them, alone, thought Bittering. No way back.

In the next days, Bittering often wandered in his garden to stand alone with his fear. As long as there were rockets he had been able to accept Mars. For always he had told himself: Tomorrow, if I want, I can buy a ticket and go back to Earth. Now they were left to the strangeness of Mars. What would happen to him, to the others? Now Mars would eat them.

He glanced up at the mountains. He thought of the old Martian names that had once been on those peaks. Earth Men dropping from the sky had gazed upon cities, hills, rivers and Martian seas left nameless. Once Martians had named all these things. Mountains melted, seas drained, cities tumbled. In spite of this the Earth Men had felt a silent guilt at putting new names to these ancient hills and valleys.

Working in the garden, he stared up at the mountains wildly and thought: Are you up there? All you dead Martians? Well, here we are, alone, cut off! Come down, move us out! We're helpless.

The wind blew a shower of peach blossoms.

He picked the blossoms up and touched them again and again.

'Cora,' he shouted, 'these blossoms!'

She handled them.

'Do you see? They're different. They've changed!'

'Look all right to me,' she said.

'They're not. They're *wrong*! I can't tell how.'

He hurried about the garden pulling up radishes, onions and carrots.

They handled the onions, radishes and carrots.

'Do they look like carrots?'

'Yes . . . No.' She hesitated. 'I don't know.'

He was afraid.

'Cora, what's happening? What is it? We've got to get away from this.'

He ran across the garden. 'The roses. The roses. They're turning green!'

And they stood looking at the green roses.

He went into town.

'Hello Harry,' said everyone.

'Look,' he said to them, 'you did hear the news the other day, didn't you?'

They nodded and laughed. 'Sure, sure, Harry.'

'What are you going to do about it?'

'Do, Harry, do? What *can* we do?'

'Build a rocket, that's what!'

'A rocket Harry? To go back to all that trouble?'

'But you must want to go back. have you noticed the peach blossoms, the onions, the grass? Doesn't it scare you?'

'Can't recall that it did much, Harry.'

Bittering wanted to cry. 'If we stay here, we'll all change. Don't you smell it? Something in the air? A Martian virus maybe; some seed or a pollen. Listen to me! Sam! Will you help me build a rocket?'

'Harry, I got a whole load of metal and some blueprints I'll sell you for five hundred dollars. You should make a right pretty rocket in about thirty years.'

Everyone laughed.

Henry Bittering moved into the metal shop and began to build the rocket. Men came and watched and joked quietly. Once in a while they gave him a hand but mostly they just idled and watched him with eyes that were slowly turning yellow coloured.

His wife appeared with food.

'I won't touch it!' he said. 'I'll eat only food from our deepfreeze that came from Earth. Nothing from our garden.'

The nights were full of wind. In the Earth Men's settlement, the Bittering house shook with a feeling of change. Lying in bed, Mr Bittering felt his bones shifted, shaped, melted like gold. His wife was burnt almost black from the sun. Dark she was, and golden-eyed and the wind roared forlorn and changing through the old peach trees, the violet grass, shaking out the green rose petals.

The fear would not be stopped.

A green star rose in the East.

He spoke a strange word: 'Iorrt. Iorrt.'

It was a Martian word. He knew no Martian.

In the middle of the night, he arose and phoned Simpson, the archaeologist.

'Simpson, what does *Iorrt* mean?'

'Why, that's the old Martian word for Earth. Why?'

'No special reason.'

A few days later, his wife told him the deepfreeze was empty. She would have to make sandwiches from food grown on Mars.

'You must eat,' she said. 'You're weak.'

He took a sandwich, opened it, looked at it, and began to nibble at it.

'And take the rest of the day off. The children want to swim in the canals. Please come along.'

The sun was hot, the day quiet. They moved along the canal. He saw the children's skin baking brown and the yellow eyes of his wife and his children that were never yellow before. But he was too tired to be afraid.

'Cora, how long have your eyes been yellow?'

'Always I guess.'

'The children's eyes are yellow too,' he said.

'Sometimes growing children's eyes change colour.'

'Maybe we're children too. At least to Mars. That's a thought.'

He laughed. 'Think I'll swim.'

Dan sat on the edge of the canal, regarding his father seriously.

'*Utha*,' he said.

'What?'

The boy smiled. 'You know. *Utha*'s the name for father in Martian.'

'Where did you learn it?'

'I don't know. Around.'

The boy hesitated. 'I – I want to change my name.'

'What's wrong with Dan?' his mother asked.

'I've a new name I want to use. Linll. Isn't it a good name? Can I use it? Can't I please?'

Mr Bittering put a hand on his head. He thought of the silly rocket, himself working alone, himself alone even among his family, so alone.

He heard his wife say, 'Why not?'

He heard himself say, 'Yes, you can use it.'

'Yaaa!' screamed the boy. 'I'm Linll, Linll!'

They walked into the hills. They came to a small deserted Martian villa on top of a hill. Blue marble halls, large murals and a swimming pool. It was refreshing in this hot summertime.

'How nice,' said Mrs Bittering, 'if we could move up here to this villa for the summer.'

'Come on,' he said, 'we're going back to town. There's work to be done on the rocket.'

But, as he worked, as the hours and days and weeks passed, the rocket receded and dwindled. The old fever was gone.

He heard the men murmuring on the porch of his metal shop.

'Everyone's going. You heard?'

Bittering came out. 'Going where?' He saw a couple of trucks, loaded with children and furniture.

'Up to the villas,' said the man. 'I'm going. What about you Harry?'

'I've got work to do here.'

'Work! You can finish that rocket in the autumn when it's cooler.'

'Got to work,' he said.

'Autumn,' they reasoned. And they sounded so sensible, so right.

Everyone worked at loading the truck in the hot, still afternoon of the next day. Laura, Dan and David carried packages. Or, as they preferred to be known, Ttill, Linnl and Werr carried the packages.

They packed little. The furniture was abandoned in the little white cottage. Somehow they did not want much of what they had brought from Earth – Laura her New York dresses, Mr Bittering his encyclopaedia, the furniture.

'I've some ideas on furniture for the villa,' he said, 'big, lazy furniture.'

The truck swung down the ancient highway out of town. There were sixty others travelling in the same direction. The town filled with a silent heavy dust from their passage. The canal lay blue in the sun and a quiet wind moved in the strange trees.

'Goodbye town,' they said, waving to it.

They did not look back again.

Summer burned the canals dry, moving like a flame on the

meadows. The painted houses flaked and peeled.

At the metal shop, the rocket frame began to rust.

In the autumn Mr Bittering stood, very dark now, very golden-eyed, upon the slope above his villa looking at the valley.

'It's time to go back,' said Cora.

'Yes, but we're not going,' he said quietly. 'There's nothing there any more. The town's empty. There's no reason to go back at all.'

Mr Bittering gazed at the Earth settlement. 'Such odd, such ridiculous houses the Earth people built.'

'They didn't know any better,' his wife said. 'Such ugly people. I'm glad they've gone.'

They both looked at each other and laughed, startled by what they had said.

'Where did they go?' he wondered. He glanced at his wife. She was golden and slender as his daughter. She looked at him, and he seemed almost as young as their eldest son.

'I'm warm. How about taking a swim?'

They turned their backs to the valley. Arm in arm they walked silently down a path of clear-running spring water.

Five years later, a rocket fell out of the sky. Men leaped out of it shouting.

'We've won the war on Earth! We're here to rescue you!'

But the town was silent. They found a flimsy rocket frame rusting in an empty shop.

They searched the hills. The lieutenant came back to report.

'The town's empty, but we found native life in the hills. Dark people. Yellow eyes. Martians. About six, eight hundred of them living in these marble ruins. Tall, healthy. Beautiful women. They haven't the foggiest notion what became of the town or its people, sir.'

'Lot's to be done, Lieutenant,' said the captain.

And his voice droned on, issuing orders, instructions, lists of tasks to be done.

But the lieutenant was gazing over the blue mountains rising beyond the canals in a quiet mist and hearing the soft wind in the air.

He was not listening.

*Ray Bradbury*
*(Adapted)*

# 15

# The First Men on Mercury

– We come in peace from the third planet. Would you take us to your leader?

– Bawr stretter! Bawr. Bawr. Stretterhawl?

– This is a little plastic model of the solar system, with working parts. You are here and we are there and we are now here with you, is this clear?

– Gawl horrop. Bawr. Abawrhannahanna!

– Where we come from is blue and white with brown, you see we call the brown here 'land', the blue is 'sea', and the white is 'clouds' over land and sea, we live on the surface of the brown land, all round is sea and clouds. We are 'men'. Men come –

– Glawp men! Gawrbenner menko. Menhawl?

– Men come in peace from the third planet which we call 'earth'. We are earthmen. Take us earthmen to your leader.

– Thmen? Thmen? Bawr. Bawrhossop. Yuleeda tan hanna. Harrabost yuleeda.

– I am the yuleeda. You see my hands, we carry no benner, we come in peace. The spaceways are all stretterhawn.

– Glawn peacemen all horrabhanna tantko! Tan come at'mstrossop. Glawp yuleeda!

– Atoms are peacegawl in our harraban. Menbat worrabost from tan hannahanna.

– You men we know bawrhossoptant. Bawr. We know yuleeda. Go strawg backspetter quick.

– We cantantabawr, tantingko backspetter now!

– Banghapper now! Yes, third planet back. Yuleeda will go back blue, white, brown nowhanna! There is no more talk.

– Gawl han fasthapper?

– No. You must go back to your planet. Go back in peace, take what you have gained but quickly.

– Stretterworra gawl, gawl . . .

– Of course, but nothing is ever the same, now is it? You'll remember Mercury.

*Edwin Morgan*

# 16

# The Fly

Shortly after noon in a remote valley of Northern Canada, a uranium prospector unslung his Geiger counter and placed it carefully on a flat rock by a patch of springy grass. For a moment he listened to its faint ticking and then switched off the current. No point in wasting the battery just to listen to the usual background chatter. So far he'd found nothing radioactive; there was no trace of uranium anywhere.

He sat down on the grass and unpacked his usual lunch of hard-boiled eggs, bread, fruit, and a flask of black coffee. He ate hungrily and when the last bite was gone he stretched out on the grass sipping at the coffee. It felt mighty good, he thought, to get off your feet after a six-hour hike through rough country.

As he lay there enjoying the strong brew, his gaze suddenly narrowed. Right before his eyes, cleverly spun between two twigs and a mossy boulder, was an intricate spider's web, its silver threads spread in a cunning network of death.

He studied it curiously, tracing with interest the special cable attached at the ends that led from the thick cushion at the web's centre to a crack in the boulder. He knew that the spider must be hidden there, crouching with one hind foot on her simple telegraph wire waiting for the vibration which would tell her that a fly was helplessly trapped among the sticky threads.

He turned his head and found her. Deep in the darkness of the crack he could just make out her sinister eyes glowing like jewels. Yes, she was at home, patient and watchful. Spiders are an ancient race, he thought: even millions of years ago they were by instinct building webs of more complex design than human engineers would ever devise.

He blinked, his attention caught once more: a glowing gem of metallic blue appeared as if from nowhere and implanted itself squarely upon the web. It was a fine specimen of a bluebottle, large, perfectly formed and brilliantly rich in colour.

He looked at the insect with surprise. It showed none of the usual panic, the frantic struggling, the shrill, terrified buzzing, but rested there in the web so calm and motionless that the spider was unaware that it was caught.

But just then the bluebottle gave a single sharp tug and a high-pitched buzz sounded. The man sighed: soon the fly would be dead. He was tempted to interfere but decided it was not for him to steal the spider's dinner and tear her web. And now she was alert. Like a pea on eight hairy, agile legs she glided swiftly over her swaying net. An age-old battle was about to be fought: the man waited with interest for the inevitable end.

About a centimetre from her prey the spider paused briefly, judging the situation with diamond-bright eyes. The man knew what would follow. The spider would have no fear of a mere fly. However large, a bluebottle was no match for a deadly spider which would without hesitation close in, secure her prey in a tangled web and drag it to her nest in the rock where she would suck out the juices at her leisure.

But instead of making a fearless attack this spider edged cautiously nearer. She seemed uneasy. The fly's strange still-ness was troubling her. The needle-pointed mandibles worked furiously.

Now, she crept forward. In a moment she would turn, squirt a jet of silk over the bluebottle and by cleverly rotating it with her hind legs, wrap it up in a gleaming shroud.

And that was exactly what she tried to do. She suddenly forgot her fears and whirled, thrusting her spinnerets towards the motionless insect.

Then the man saw an incredible thing. There was a metallic flash and a shining steel-like rod shot from the fly's head and pierced the spider's plump underbelly where it remained forming a deadly bond.

The spider stiffened as the deadly lance struck home. Now she was rigid, paralysed, her swollen belly pulsing in and out as the fly drained away the vital juices.

It was impossible! How could a fly kill a spider? But then was it really a fly? Insects often mimic each other. But no, there was no mistaking it. As he peered closer he could clearly see that it was a bluebottle.

Raising himself to his knees he looked more closely at the fly. It seemed as if that deadly weapon came not from the mouth but through a small hatch-like opening between the bulging eyes. But that was absurd! Suddenly, with a quick flickering motion, the rod retracted. The opening was gone. Shrivelled to a husk, the spider still stood upright on her thin legs.

One thing was certain to the prospector: he must capture this remarkable fly which fortunately was stuck fast in the web. Knowing the steely toughness of those silken strands he realised that killing the spider would not save it: very few insects ever tear free. He gingerly extended his thumb and forefinger. Easy now. . . . He must pull the fly loose without crushing it.

Then he stopped, almost touching the insect, and stared hard. Just as the spider had been, he was now uneasy – a little frightened. A bright, glowing spot, brilliant even in the glaring sunlight, throbbed on the very tip of the blue abdomen and a faint whine came from the trapped insect.

Excited, he reached forward again, but as his fingers approached, the fly rose smoothly in a vertical climb tearing a gap through the web. Quickly the man cupped his hand and snapped it shut over the insect. The captive buzzed furiously within his grasp. Suddenly he yelped in agony as a burning pain scalded his palm. He relaxed his grip. There was a streak of electric blue as the fly soared away glinting in the sun. For an instant he saw again that faint light at its tail, a dazzling spark against the darker sky. Then nothing.

He examined the wound in his hand swearing bitterly. It was purple, and although little blisters had already formed, there was no sign of a puncture. Seemingly the creature had not used a sting but merely spurted venom – an acid perhaps – onto his skin. Certainly the injury felt very much like a bad burn. Blast! He'd lost a real find – an insect not yet known to science. With a little more care he might have caught it.

Stiff and angry with himself, he got sullenly to his feet and repacked his lunch kit. He reached for the Geiger counter, switched on the power, took one step towards a distant outcrop of rock – and froze. The slight background rattle of the Geiger had increased to a deafening staccato. He stood there looking puzzled and then took his hand away. The Geiger counter returned to its normal ticking. He waited trying to understand what had happened and suddenly his eyes lit up with a fearful understanding. Gently he reached out his blistered palm to the machine . . . and the Geiger counter roared again!

*Arthur Porges*
(Adapted)

# 17

# Chocky

We were still trying to make up our minds the next Tuesday. That was the day I stopped on the way home to take delivery of a new car. It was a station-wagon that I'd been hankering after for some time. Lots of room for everyone, and for a load of gear in the back as well. We all piled in, and took it out for a short experimental run before supper. I was pleased with the way it handled and thought I'd get to like it. The others were enthusiastic, and by the time we returned it was generally voted that the Gore family was entitled to tilt its chins a degree or two higher.

I left the car parked in front of the garage ready to take Mary and me to a friend's house later on, and went to write a letter while Mary got the supper.

About a quarter of an hour later came the sound of Matthew's raised voice. I couldn't catch what he was saying; it was a noise of half-choked, inarticulate protest. Looking out of the window I noticed that several passers-by had paused and were looking over the gate with expressions of uncertain amusement. I went out to investigate. I found Matthew standing a few feet from the car, very red in the face, and shouting incoherently. I walked towards him.

'What's the trouble, Matthew?' I inquired.

He turned. There were tears of childish rage running down his flushed cheeks. He tried to speak, but choked on the words, and grabbed my hand with both of his. I looked at the car which seemed to be the focus of the trouble. It did not appear damaged, nor to have anything visibly amiss with it. Then, conscious of the spectators at the gate, I led Matthew round to the other side of the house, out of their sight. There I sat down on one of the veranda chairs, and took him on my knee. I had never seen him so upset. He was shaking with anger, half-strangled by it, and still with tears copiously streaming. I put an arm round him.

'There now, old man. Take it easy. Take it easy,' I told him.

Gradually the shaking and the tears began to subside. He breathed more easily. By degrees the tension in him relaxed, and he grew quieter. After a time he heaved a great, exhausted sigh. I handed him my handkerchief. He plied it a bit, and then he blew.

'Sorry, Daddy,' he apologized through it, still chokily.

'That's all right, old man. Just take your time.'

Presently he lowered the handkerchief and plucked at it, still breathing jerkily. A few more tears, but of a different kind, overflowed. He cleaned up once more, sighed again, and began to be more like his normal self.

'Sorry, Daddy,' he said again. 'All right now – I think.'

'Good,' I told him. 'But dear, oh dear, what was all that about?'

Matthew hesitated, then he said,

'It was the car.'

I blinked.

'The car! For heaven's sake. It seems to be all right. What's it done to you?'

'Well, not the car, exactly,' Matthew amended. 'You see, it's a jolly nice car, I think it's super, and I thought Chocky would be interested in it, so I started showing it to her, and telling her how it works, and things.'

I became aware of a slight sinking, here-we-go-again feeling.

'But Chocky wasn't interested?' I inquired.

Something seemed to rise in Matthew's throat, but he took himself in hand, swallowed hard and continued bravely:

'She said it was silly, and ugly, and clumsy. She – she *laughed* at it!'

At the recollection of this enormity his indignation swelled once more, and all but overwhelmed him. He strove to fight it down.

I asked: 'What does she find so amusing about it?'

Matthew sniffed, paused, and sniffed again.

'Pretty nearly everything,' he told me, gloomily. 'She said the engine is funny, and old-fashioned, and wasteful, and that an engine that needed gears was ridiculous anyway. And that a car that didn't use an engine to stop itself as well as make itself go was stupid. And how it was terribly funny to think of anyone making a car that had to have springs because it just bumped along the ground on wheels that had to have things like sausages fastened round them.

'So I told her that's how cars are, anyway, and ours is a new car, and a jolly good one. And she said that was non-sense because our car is just silly, and nobody with any brains would make anything so clumsy and dangerous, and

nobody with any sense would ride in one. And then – well, it's a bit muddled after that because I got angry. But, anyway, I don't care what *she* thinks: I *like* our new car.'

'What does she think cars ought to be like, then?' I asked.

'That's what *I* asked her when she started on our car,' said Matthew. 'And she said that where she comes from the cars don't have wheels at all. They go along a bit above the ground, and they don't make any noise, either. She said that our kind of cars that have to keep to roads are bound to run into one another pretty often, and that, anyway, properly made cars are made so that they *can't* run into one another.'

'There's quite a lot to be said for that – if you can manage it,' I admitted. 'But, tell me, where *does* Chocky come from?' Matthew frowned.

'That's one of the things we can't find out,' he said. 'It's too difficult. You see, if you don't know where anything else is, how can you find out where you are?'

'You mean, no reference points?' I suggested.

'I expect that's it,' Matthew said, a little vaguely. 'But I think where Chocky lives must be a very, very long way away. *Everything* seems to be different there.'

'H'm,' I said. I tried another tack. 'How old is Chocky?' I asked.

'Oh, pretty old,' Matthew told me. 'Her time doesn't go like ours though. But we worked it out that if it did she'd be at least twenty. Only she says she'll go on living until she's about two hundred, so that sort of makes twenty seem less. She thinks only living until you're seventy or eighty like we do, is silly and wasteful.'

'Chocky,' I suggested, 'appears to think a great many things silly.'

Matthew nodded emphatically.

'Oh, she does,' he agreed. 'Nearly everything, really,' he added, in amplification.

'Rather depressing,' I commented.

'It does get a bit boring pretty often,' Matthew conceded.

Then Mary called us in to supper.

*John Wyndham*

# 18

# Grinny

Jan. 14

Astonishing news! I had come back from Mac's house and had just been shouted at as usual by Mum (TAKE YOUR BOOTS OFF) when I heard the station taxi grinding up the drive and soon after, our bell being rung. I was still in the porch so I opened the door and *there she was*, all five feet one of her, with two gi-normous trunks. I did not know what to say, but she said, 'I am your Great Aunt Emma. You must be Tim,' and I mumbled something about calling Mother, but Mum had heard the bell go and came hurtling along the corridor shouting, 'If it's the Guides, it must wait till Tuesday and if it's Mac, tell him to TAKE HIS BOOTS OFF.' When she goes to heaven, she will say this to all the archangels.

I said, 'It's Great Aunt Emma, Mum, were you expecting — ?' but she simply said, '*Most* amusing, you *witty* lad!' in her Wednesday matinée voice and went belting past on her way to the kitchen. Then she caught a glimpse of Aunt Emma and stopped in her tracks and came to the doorway. '*Who*?' she said. 'Great Aunt *who*?' I could see she was completely foxed and had never heard of GAE,  as I will henceforth refer to Great Aunt Emma, as she is bound to figure largely in these pages from now on.

GAE said, 'You remember me, Millie!' but Mum could only see a vague shape and replied, 'Oh dear, I am afraid I don't quite remember – ?' Then I switched on the porch light and Mum could see GAE properly. GAE leaned forward and said again, 'You remember me, Millie!' and this time the penny dropped and Mum cried out, 'Great Aunt Emma! Oh do come in, you must be freezing. Tim, help with the luggage!'

So we got her inside and she is rather a queer old party. Very short, with a hat with a veil, and gloves, and a way of smiling vaguely. Her teeth are very good (false?) and she is very neat. Her shoes hardly have creases in them over the instep, as if she never walked, yet she is quite spry considering her age and soon she and Mum were chattering away about the journey and so on. At first Mum didn't seem quite with the situation, I could tell she was faking a lot, but she is

42

such a good faker (unlike Father) that only an outsider could have told that she was a bit baffled by GAE. Anyhow, this soon passed, I saw her (Mum) wipe the back of her hand across her brow which is always a sign that her mind is now made up and Into Action! After another few minutes you could have sworn that Mum had been expecting GAE for the last fortnight, that the bed was aired and so on. She is very good at that sort of thing.

Then Father and Beth came in from feeding the rabbits. He made a complete bosh of it as usual, saying all the wrong things and making it quite clear that he hadn't a clue about the very existence of Great Aunts. But she fixed him with her beady eye, and grinned, and said, 'You remember me, Edward!' and he re-entered the twentieth century in great style, pouring everyone sherry. He gave Beth (who is seven) as much sherry as me (eleven) which is typical. Beth was as ever the Outstanding Social Success and shook hands and said, 'Oh what a lovely surprise,' and looked more like a telly ad. than ever. I suppose it's a graceful accomplishment, but it's also the mark of a little cow. She swallowed the sherry pretty fast and went across to pour herself some more but Mum caught her eye and said 'Beth . . . !' and that was the end of that. I got another half glass later. It is quite good sherry, a Manzanilla.

Mum drew me aside and of course it was me that had to go and put hot water bottles in the spare bed and turn on the heaters and so on to get the room ready for GAE. When I got back to the living-room they were all talking away. GAE obviously has a knack for social chitchat, she just asks questions that set people talking again. When I came in, she said, 'Tim, are you old enough to smoke?' I said no, of course, although I have smoked (what a ridiculous habit). She said, 'I am so glad, now I won't have to be polite and offer you one of these horrid things. I have only four left.' She pulled out a packet of Gauloises and lit one – she had already had one, the stub was in an ashtray – and said, 'Let me see, are you fourteen or fifteen, Tim?'

I felt myself turning pink at this ridiculous question and mumbled, 'Eleven. Nearly twelve.' Sure enough, Beth said, 'But he's old enough to shave, Aunt Emma!' in her Sweet Little Girl voice and everyone began to say What shave When shave Why shave Who shave How shave, just as Beth intended. What makes it all worse is that I tried Father's shaving things that time simply out of curiosity, not to prove myself a great hairy man or anything stupid like that. But of course as Father is always reminding me, WAW, Women Always Win.

Anyhow, what an absurd thing to ask me if I am fourteen or fifteen, quite obviously I am not. If GAE thought she was flattering me, wrong guess. I tried to cover up by asking her how old she was. Beth murmured, 'How rude' – another point to her – but GAE said, 'I have been sixty-nine now for more years than I care to remember,' and everyone laughed politely.

So it went on like that and she eventually went off to bed in high style. Thank heaven she is not a kisser, just a peck-on-the-cheeker. When Aunt Lilian was here, saying good night was like those old movies with sobbing violins.

Will get Beth somehow.

Jan. 15

GAE no fool. I wonder how old she really is? Very alert and always asking questions, most of them good. Asked Father WHY he wanted to know about Roman settlement below undercroft and he lost another three minutes telling her. Most women merely think his work Quaint, like that woman who kept saying, 'So historical!' but GAE wants to know what it's all for. Kept asking even when Father gone, so not just faking.

GAE asked where she could get more French ciggies, saw Mum flinch (though she does not mind them as much as ordinary fags). Told her only one place, Tillots in the village, and even then she would be lucky (she was – they did stock them). She said would I take her, had to say yes. So we walked there, me dreading slow tottering steps and having to hang back. But she kept going at a fair old pace. Very cold, nose dripping (mine not hers – She didn't even mention cold). Funny really, she wore black long coat, black boots, black hat with fur and veil again. Said it kept her face warm. I said something about the early days of motoring and women wearing veils then but she said she didn't remember and started asking me about cars. What is a sports car for, she asked, and I said, to go faster. How much faster? I said not really much faster, in fact some saloons were faster than some sports cars. Then why did people buy sports cars? Etc., etc. Lots more of this sort. Questions that made *me* think. I told her about electric cars but (as we found out later) GAE hates anything electric, which is one of the odd, old-ladyish things about her. She seems to think that anything electrical could *leak* electricity . . . she flinches away from electric fires, irons, anything.

Funny that she asks all these questions at her age, I suppose old people get a second wind when they start looking at life all over again and asking all the questions they didn't ask when they were young. She never talks about the past.

All in all, rather enjoyed the walk and certainly she's a good goer – quite unpuffed on return, lit a Gauloise and read paper right through without a further word.

Jan. 20

Muscle Beach[1] this morning, Father a bit hearty, saying 'Swimming in January! There's luxury!' Beth as usual moaning and ending up by crying 'It's NOT luxury! It's NOT luxury!' which made Father and me laugh. We stripped and dived in, horrible anticipation but very nice once done. Water 67°. Father ploughing up and down doing his 30 lengths, very stern and dutiful, but must admit he looks better than most men of his age. E.g. cannot imagine Dr Parry (six years younger than Father) stripped to the buff, must be obscene. Physician, heal thyself.

Beth doing her amazing breaststroke, head and bottom sticking out of water, mouth going 'Pouf! Pouf!', eyes closed most of the time.

I did length underwater, then two lengths = 50 feet. Nearly burst lungs.

Mother as usual found excuse, did not come. Yet she is far best swimmer. My theory – she never really approves of the naked bit. Is it her appendicitis scar? Probably. She is quite vain and I don't blame her as very pretty considering age (34). She moans about the scar – surgeon was a butcher etc., etc. – but not seriously. But she does mention it. I read an article in the paper the other day that said all this modern thing about families romping around naked and unashamed

---

[1]Muscle Beach – the Carpenter's swimming-pool, built by Mr Carpenter. It has a removable glass roof and is heated for winter use. The pool is Mr Carpenter's greatest luxury, the only item, he says, on which he has ever spent more than he can afford – and the only thing, his work apart, about which he is somewhat fanatical and insistent. He uses the pool daily and makes it plain that he expects the family to follow his example at weekends, even in darkest winter.

*The Author*

was a snare and a delusion. I must say I never thought about it at all, the swimming-pool was just a thing we had and it's always been there – since I was four anyhow – and you don't wear clothes in your own swimming-pool although you do in someone else's or on the beach. No one in our house goes around naked indoors or leaves loo door open. But since the Permissive Scene came on, you can't even brush your teeth without feeling that you've got to prove something. I wish I was Father, who simply doesn't comment – just does what he wants to do. But of course, even that's all changed now because of GAE, viz –

There we are splashing in the pool when – ker-doing! – door opens, icy blast ruffles water, and lo! GAE has come among us, wearing gumboots and mild grin! All is instantly confusion! The great traditions hallowed by the Carpenter family are shaken to the corblimey! – particularly the tradition whereby Muscle Beach = unembarrassed starkers. Beth is least affected – she merely says Eeek!, then recovers herself and goes on with her rotten breaststroke, this time with her eyes open to see how dear Papa and dear Brother take the situation.

I zoom out of the pool at the far end and slide like a seal into a towel in one easy movement. So I am now unnaked and therefore unashamed. Not trendy, but true.

But Father is visibly taken aback. He stops swimming, stands in the middle of the pool and says 'Oh.' Then he adds, 'Aunt Emma. Oh. Good morning.' And, trying to look unconcerned, completes his thirty lengths. But he's concerned all right, because instead of doing racing turns at either end, which he learned with great labour from the swimmers on TV, he now turns in the modest amateur hand-push manner: the difference being that the amateur manner just causes a swirl of water round his shoulder while the racing turn shows his *bottom*.

At last he can swim no longer and once again he stands in the middle of the pool and says, in an abnormally normal voice, 'Oh, good morning, Aunt Emma. You're up bright and early.'

She looks out through the glass overhead as if to check the truth of his statement and replies 'Yes indeed' – then calmly sits down and stares at Father, waiting for him to say something else.

Taking the bull by the horns, he says, 'Well, cough cough, that's enough swimming for me, hum hum, I think I will get out now.'

Aunt Emma says, 'Yes indeed.'

Father's eyes flick first to Beth, who deliberately turns her back to him and duck-dives; then to me – but I pretend to have my arms caught in a sweater. Seeing that he will get no support from his nearest and dearest, Father says, loud and clear, 'You must leave now, Aunt Emma, I'm getting out.'

'Oh,' says Aunt Emma, the grin fading. 'Why?'

'Because I'm not wearing anything!' Father grates.

'I should hope not,' says Aunt Emma. *It would only get wet!*

I was going to go on to examine this situation in depth, but it's too good to spoil and I am sleepy. So I will leave him in the water, facing Aunt Emma (still seated) and laugh myself to sleep.

Feb. 9

This is not easy to write. I know I send up Beth all the time and make jokes about WAW and so on and she is after all only a seven-year-old (but soon to be eight) – but she is nothing like such a fool as I like to make her out to be and if she is a liar, she is doing it very well – even crying with the lying. I don't know what to make of it.

She was sitting in her room and refusing to come down. Eventually Mum sent me up to tell Beth that dinner was nearly on the table and that she really must come down. I crashed into Beth's room and said, 'Oh, come on, Beth, it's dinner time and I've had to come all the way upstairs,' etc., etc. She just burst into tears and said she wasn't coming down, she refused to come down, leave me alone and so on.

She looked so awful that I didn't start on her in the usual way but tried to be nice – what's wrong, did something happen at school, aren't you well. She said, 'No, no, it's her – Grinny! It's Grinny!' Anyhow, Mum was standing at the foot of the stairs yelling for us to come down so I pulled her (Beth) to her feet and said, 'Will you tell me after?' and she replied, 'Yes, but only if you promise!' Which means of course promise not to tell anyone else.

She was quiet and white at dinner but I don't think anyone took much notice as there were two men from the site, a stonemason and a photographer, having a meal with us and they and Father kept talking shop at the top of their voices all the time. Beth ate as much as usual. But as soon as the meal was over and we had cleared the dishes, she tugged at my arm and made me go back with her to her room.

She said, 'I've been longing to tell someone, but they'll only laugh. Will you laugh?' I said no. She said, 'Do you think I am just a stupid little girl or don't you? Because I'm not.' She started crying again so I gave her the old hug and kiss treatment, which I don't often do, so when I do do it it works all the better (*do do it it* is like a word puzzle). It worked now – she stopped crying, stared me straight in the face and said –

'*Grinny's not real.*'

I said, 'Oh.' I was disappointed in her for being so childish, actually.

She said, 'Yes, I knew you would take it like that, you just think I'm stupid, but I am not. *Grinny is not real*, she's not a real person at all.'

It went on like this for a litle while, then I said. 'Tell me exactly and precisely what you are talking about and no messing about and above all do not cry.'

She said, 'You remember the day she fell down on the ice and hurt herself?' I said yes. 'Well, I was the first one there, I was there just about a second after she did it, she was still lying on the ground and I was there beside her. And I saw something you will never believe, never!'

I said what was it and I would try to believe her.

She said, 'Something horrible, it was *horrible*! I saw her wrist actually broken and the bone sticking out!'

I replied, 'That's impossible. Do be reasonable, she was perfectly all right quite soon after. If you break your wrist it is very serious, it takes weeks or months to mend. Particularly if you are old. And it is very painful, agony, in fact. So you just couldn't have seen it, Beth, you only thought you saw it because you have a good imagination.'

Beth said, 'I haven't got a good imagination, Penny writes much better essays than I do and so does Sue. I saw it, I saw it, I saw it!'

So I made her tell me just what it was she saw. She started off by repeating that I would never believe her and so on, but in the end it came down to this – I am choosing my words very carefully so as not to distort what she said –

'She was lying on the ground in a heap. She was not groaning or moaning, just lying there and kicking her legs, trying to get up. I went close to her and got hold of her elbow so that I could help pull her up. She did not say anything to me, like "Help me" or "My wrist hurts" – she just tried to get up. When I seized her elbow, I saw her wrist. The hand was dangling. The wrist was so badly broken that the skin was all cut open in a gash and the bones were showing.'

I told Beth I understood all this, but she seemed unwilling to go on. She looked at me and wailed, 'Oh, it's no good, you'll never believe me!' but I made her go on. She said:

'*The skin was gashed open but there was no blood. The bones stuck out but they were not made of real bone – they were made of shiny steel!*'

I have these words right. Beth did say what I have written. I am quite certain about asking her what sort of bones, what sort of steel and so on. Her answers were, that the steel was silvery shiny and that the bones looked smaller than proper bones – more like umbrella ribs. When I asked her what umbrella ribs look like, she answered (correctly) that they are made of channels of steel, not solid rods like knitting needles. She said that GAE's bones were in 'little collections' of these steel ribs and that the skin had been torn by a few of the ribs breaking away from a main cluster and coming through the skin.

So I asked her again about the absence of blood and she was positive. She said there was no blood, no blood at all, the skin was just split open. I asked her what colour the skin was and she said the same colour outside as in. I said, well, there must have been meaty stuff where the bones were, but she said no. There was nothing but the steel ribs and that the skin was just a thick layer 'like the fat on a mutton chop before it is cooked', but with a tear in it.

I thought of all kinds of reasons for her telling this story, ranging from my linocut set, which has very sharp (= frightening) gouges, some of them the same section as umbrella ribs; right down to playing in the garden when we were much younger with an old tattered umbrella, all spokes and no cover (it was pelting with rain and we were making a joke of the useless umbrella, etc., etc.).

As I was thinking of all the things that might have caused Beth to think she saw what she said she saw, she began again. 'I saw her wrist mend! I saw it heal itself!' she said.

I must say, this gave me goosepimples. I said, 'What do you mean?' and Beth told me that as she watched, *the skin came together over the broken bones leaving a bump covering the breaks*. That was when Beth became really frightened and ran inside.

I said to her, 'You know that people actually can have metal bones?' She said, 'Oh yes, I've always known that and so have you. Father nearly had one, you remember.' I did remember – he broke a bone and the hospital thought that he might have to have a steel rod inserted to pin the bone. In the end he didn't. Some people do, however, and it may be permanent. A man in the village has a metal plate in his skull.

So it is no good me trying to pretend that Beth has some fixation or other about bones and umbrella ribs because she simply hasn't. Cream, coffee, chocolates, chicken and stuffing – she's certainly got fixations about them. But not people's bones.

By now she was saying, 'I told you! I knew all along you wouldn't believe me!' and preparing to have a good cry again. I managed to avoid this by more kiss and hug treatment and in the end I said, 'All right, so Grinny has an artificial arm, let's say, made by some super surgeon. For all we know, she's got false teeth, wears a wig, has a cork leg and a glass eye. Fine! But what difference does it make? Why get upset and refuse to kiss her good night and all the rest of it?'

Beth set up a great howl and shouted 'Oh, how can you be so stupid! It's nothing to do with false legs and glass eyes – IT'S BECAUSE SHE'S NOT REAL, that's why I can't stand her.

50

NONE OF HER IS REAL!'

She was making such a row that I said, 'All right, all right, I understand now. And then of course you don't like the way she smells and it all adds up in your mind –'

Beth went very white and said, 'Yes, and she doesn't smell of anything, that's another thing! And she asks those stupid questions! And she's frightened of electricity! It all proves it, she's not real!'

I quietened her down eventually (she had started crying again in a very big way) and let her come into my room while I did my homework. She was fairly happy by her bedtime. But I must admit she has put the frighteners on me. I am writing this rather late and I keep expecting a crack to appear in the wall, then a hole, then a metal hand come through the plaster. That sort of thing. A good story might be written about a metal hand.

I just do not know what to make of it all. Beth's only a little girl but she is *not* an idiot.

*Nicholas Fisk*

# 19

# The Marrog

My desk's at the back of the class
　　And nobody, nobody knows
　　　　I'm a Marrog from Mars
With a body of brass
　　And seventeen fingers and toes.

Wouldn't they shriek if they knew
　　I've three eyes at the back of my head
　　　　And my hair is bright purple
My nose is deep blue
　　And my teeth are half-yellow, half-red.

My five arms are silver, and spiked
　　With knives on them sharper than spears.
I could go back right now, if I liked –
　　And return in a million light-years.

I could gobble them all,
For I'm seven foot tall
　　And I'm breathing green flames from my ears.

Wouldn't they yell if they knew,
　　If they guessed that a Marrog was here?
Ha-ha, they haven't a clue –
　　Or wouldn't they tremble with fear!
'Look, look a Marrog'
　　They'd all scream – and SMACK
The blackboard would fall and the ceiling would crack
　　And teacher would faint, I suppose.
But I grin to myself, sitting right at the back
　　And nobody, nobody knows.

*R.C. Scriven*

# 20

# Alien Contact

## THE UNIVERSE IS A VERY BIG PLACE

Take a bus, train or car into the country. Even from the centre of the largest city on Earth it will take you only a few hours. If you find yourself in flat country gaze from horizon to horizon. The wide open spaces look vast, yet you are probably only seeing a few miles in any direction. If you find yourself in hill country or in the mountains, take the trouble to climb a hill. The view may seem magnificent, and the world may seem bigger, but it is unlikely that you will see further than fifty miles and the planet Earth is a much bigger place than that. To measure its circumference you would need a tape measure twenty-four-thousand miles long!

Imagine you are an astronaut halfway on a voyage to the moon. From forty-thousand miles away the planet Earth is a blue sphere marbled white with cloud, a spaceship Earth for every human being and every animal and every plant, for all the living things of the entire solar system. Among the planets of our sun only Earth has life.

The sun is a star, a small bright star 92 million miles from Earth. On a bright, clear night look up at the sky. Look at the infinite multitude of stars, the millions of suns of the Milky Way orbiting around the galaxy, a million, million stars in motion, trailing countless millions of planets. They are all very far away. The nearest star is so far away that if you were to travel at the speed of light, 186 thousand miles per second, it would take you not one minute, not one hour, not one whole day to reach it, but over four years of constant travel. Alpha centauri is four light years away.

And beyond this galaxy and its million, million stars lie other galaxies, separated from ours by even greater distances, some larger, some smaller, clusters of galaxies stretching in all directions as far as our telescopes can probe, a billion, billion galaxies, the debris of the explosion with which it all began.

The universe is a very big place.

# WE ARE NOT ALONE!

We are not alone. In such an enormous universe are many alien races who have achieved the high technology to travel through space. Many are far in advance of us – and before the twentieth-century was to close we were destined to have our first real contact with such an alien people, a contact that would both frighten us and flatter us, for they came not to attack us but to ask for our help. They came as refugees, fleeing from a tyranny, deeper and more terrible than we could ever imagine in our darkest nightmares.

They called themselves the 'People of the White Flame'.

So, when they came, they were not alone; for they were pursued through the star systems of our galaxy by their enemies, another alien race, fierce and greedy for new territories, new planets to conquer and subdue. For many months the People of the White Flame had lived with fear, anxiously checking their instruments, scanning their hateful enemies as they drew closer and closer until capture seemed inevitable. Their power systems were fading, their stocks of food running low, their recycled water supply all but finished and they were still many light years from the protection of their own planetary system. Two hundred million miles from Earth and approaching, they were far beyond the frontiers of their star charts. Ahead lay the unknown, the unexplored spiral of the galaxy with its scattered suns.

And then they found us, a new civilisation, a new technology, young in years but perhaps just sufficiently advanced to help them on their way before their enemies closed in for the kill – perhaps just friendly enough and generous enough to give the aid they so desperately needed.

Perhaps . . .

## RAF Early-warning base

RED ALERT!    RED ALERT!    RED ALERT!    RED ALERT!    RED ALERT!

Large, unidentified object approaching from polar region. Possible hostile missile. Altitude, 120 miles. Velocity, 17500 m.p.h.

Washington confirms readings from Greenland. Only one missile so far detected. NATO Red Alert initiated.

Scramble Tornadoes. Polaris deployed. Trident deployed. Cruise deployed.

Alert BBC for Doomsday Newsflash.

Object now in stationary orbit over North Atlantic.

Carrier Jefferson of US Navy now co-ordinating investigation.

Prime Minister contacted.

Fall-out shelters activated.

Object measured as ten miles long.

Soviet air activity detected over North Cape.

Hotline in use – Moscow – Washington – London – Paris.

NATO stand down. Warsaw Pact stand down.

## The Daily Review

### Foreign Secretary speaks of mystery object

At 10 o'clock last night the Foreign Secretary finally confirmed rumours which had been gathering all day regarding a huge unidentified object which had parked in stationary orbit over the North Atlantic. In a short statement the Foreign Secretary, Alice Clements, admitted that as yet a full explanation was impossible. She assured the country that there was no cause for alarm.

All day there had been exchanges between our NATO allies and close consultation with President Gilbert of the USA who is taking the matter very seriously. Ms Clements admitted that the Hotline to Moscow had been used frequently since the start of the crisis. (It was the first time the word 'crisis' had been used by a member of the Government.) Chairman Markov would be making a statement to the Russian people later that evening.

Ms. Clements stressed that there was now no question of the object being a hostile device from the Soviet Union and it was certainly not from the West. As far as could be determined it posed no military threat.

Astronomers were divided as to its origin, some claiming that it was not a natural phenomenon. Asked if the mystery object could be of extra-terrestrial origin, the Foreign Secretary declined to comment. She left immediately for another meeting with the Prime Minister.

### Littleton School Space Scoop

Science master, Brian Craven of Littleton Techno School claims that he has monitored distinct radio emissions from the mystery object over the North Atlantic.

Over a period of six hours he and senior pupils of the school recorded several bursts of radio pulses which were not consistent with natural phenomena. He is convinced that the authorities know more than they care to tell us at this stage. Asked if he could decipher any of the pulses, Mr Craven replied, 'It's too early yet, but one thing I am sure of, whoever put that thing together is intelligent, very intelligent. It is definitely not a captured meteor as some astronomers are suggesting.'

### Greenwich Observatory Sighting

Astronomers at the Royal Observatory at Greenwich have made their first statement about the mystery object. Through clear skies at one o'clock this morning they caught their first sighting of the mysterious intruder by telescope and were able to make some measurements. Professor Manson said they were astounded by their findings. The object was cylindrical in shape, tapering at either end and at first estimate an astonishing twelve miles in length. It appeared to have smooth shiny sides along which flickering lights were clearly visible. From time to time smaller objects seemed to emerge from it, travelling at incredible speeds in various directions before disappearing.

## 12 APRIL 1995          ALIEN CONTACT DAY THREE

### Headlines for the day – What the papers say

*Daily Reflector*

'WE COME IN PEACE' –
BUT BUG-EYED SPACE BUDDIES BEG FOR HELP!

*Daily Review*

WE ARE NOT ALONE! CONTACT AT LAST!
– AND THEY'RE FRIENDLY!

*Daily Telstar*

FIRST ALIEN CONTACT SUCCESSFUL.
P.M. STATES, 'THERE HAVE BEEN POSITIVE EXCHANGES'

## Transcript of a message from the First Lord of the 'People of the White Flame'

To the Governments and People
of the Planet Earth in the Outer Sector

WE COME IN PEACE,
WE COME FOR HELP.
WE ARE PURSUED BY THE ENEMY.

We require raw materials, protein, water and engineering services. Without these we cannot continue our journey to our home planet. We may be subdued by our terrible enemy, the Dark Lord of the Silent Star Fleets. If he subdues us, he will not stop until your whole planet is under his subjection.

If you help us to escape we will offer you contact with our civilisation at the centre of the galaxy and you will have our complete protection.

We shall give you music of great beauty such as you have never heard before. You will share our culture and enjoy works of art you have not dreamt of. Your hearts will be filled with joy. Your minds will be enlarged with new experiences. we shall teach you new truths, new sciences, new arts and life will begin again for you and all the children of your planet. There will be no more hunger and no more pain. There will be abundant life and grief will cease in your lands.

We have three months by your reckoning before the ships of the Dark Lord close in upon us and enslave us all to his evil purpose. If, by your help, we escape within that time we shall lead them away from you and leave you safely shielded. And we shall come again in happier times and our promises shall be fulfilled.

# CABINET MEETING

## Problems for the World . . .
## Problems for Britain . . .

The request for help from the alien people presents both the world in general and His Majesty's Government here in Britain with a number of problems. In coming to a decision the following points should be considered:

a. The request from the 'People of the White Flame' for assistance has gone to the world in general. It is not directed at specific countries. The world, however, is divided. There are vast differences between the rich, technically advanced countries and the poor, developing countries. The only countries capable of rendering effective assistance to the aliens are the powerful, technically advanced countries mainly of the North, the USA, Europe, and the Soviet Union.

b. The present tension in the world and the arms race between NATO and the Warsaw Pact makes it difficult to establish an agreement on a common policy for assisting aliens. Both sides will almost certainly try to exploit the situation in order to gain advantage in military technology. Extreme caution must be adopted. An alliance between the Warsaw Pact and the 'People of the White Flame' could have disastrous consequences for the Western Alliance, but obviously the East would view a NATO–Alien alliance as equally undesirable.

c. We must also question the alien assertion that they are being pursued by a ruthless enemy. This may only be a ruse to gain our confidence and sympathy and so put us at a disadvantage. We require extra time to test the trustworthiness of the aliens and to examine their promises in detail. The wording of their first message is rather vague. If their story is true, however, we may not have sufficient time since they claim their enemies are only months away. Alternatively, the alien story may be only partly true. They have presented their enemies as evil. What if it is the other way around? We may find ourselves helping the wrong side and become enslaved to an alien and hostile civilization.

# CABINET MEETING

## British Policy

After receiving advice from the Foreign Office on the British position in the Alien Crisis, the Prime Minister and Cabinet decided on the following policy:

1. Before any final decision is taken to help the aliens, Britain will try to act jointly with the USA and the USSR to establish a treaty of mutual benefit for all the countries of the world. This could be administered through the agency of the United Nations. If this fails, Britain will 'go it alone'.

2. Representatives of the 'People of the White Flame' will be invited to Britain for discussions at the Foreign Office.

3. A request will be made for the Prime Minister to visit the alien spacecraft in orbit to assess their sincerity and good will. He will be accompanied by technical advisers, including military, in order to find out what exactly the aliens have to offer.

4. A technical advisory committee will be set up immediately to draw up a list of Britain's most vital technological needs for presentation to the aliens.

5. All British Intelligence agencies will be constantly updated on the developing situation.

## The Prime Minister's Special TV Broadcast

At three o'clock this afternoon I had an audience with His Majesty at Buckingham Palace. There I was able to give him a full account of the Government's actions and decisions since the arrival in Earth's orbit of a large spacecraft flown by alien creatures who refer to themselves as the 'People of the White Flame'.

I now have to tell you with deep regret that all attempts on our part to secure international agreement for assisting the aliens and sharing their gifts have met with total failure.

Yesterday I visited the craft in orbit and spent several hours in fruitful conversation with their First Lord. I came away convinced of their sincerity and I have been able to persuade my fellow cabinet ministers likewise. Consequently we have decided to adopt a policy of 'go it alone' whatever America or Russia may decide.

Tomorrow at noon Greenwich Mean Time the First Lord will touch down in his shuttle craft in Hyde Park and will be conveyed to Buckingham Palace to meet His Majesty.

You may be assured that we will render our friends in space every assistance and will rigorously repel any attempts by other nations to prevent this. In doing this we have clearly set an example to the other nations of this planet and our actions will greatly benefit the people of this country.

Thank you and goodnight.

# DEPARTURE

*Transcript of radio broadcast describing the official departure of the 'People of the White Flame' from Britain.*

And so the day has finally come, the day our alien friends, the 'People of the White Flame' as they style themselves, must take their leave of us. They came in friendship and trust seeking help and now, even with their dreaded enemies speeding towards them in pursuit, they pause this day to give us an official thanks, here at Hyde Park, before embarking.

And it is here that the crowds have been gathering since early yesterday evening to pay their respects and to wish these splendid aliens a safe journey through the measureless star systems to their home on the other side of the galaxy, to the planet which takes its name from the great white sun that sustains it.

And now, the sun is rising. From where I am standing I can see its first golden rays reflecting from the intensely polished surfaces of the alien shuttle that will take the last representatives of the White Flame People back to their gigantic spacecraft still in orbit over the North Atlantic. The shuttle is like a large, slightly flattened cigar, as smooth as a globule of water, without even the appearance of windows or portholes, though I can vouch that from the interior windows do indeed exist. I was privileged to make a trip in it last month with a BBC camera-crew and I know that many of you will by now be familiar with the incredible film that we took.

To the north of the shuttle a platform has been built to accommodate the farewell ceremony. From it extends a straight red carpet right up to the entry ports of the shuttle. On my monitor I can see that the first distinguished guests have arrived and taken their places. I can see the Archbishop of Canterbury and Cardinal Andrews of the Roman Catholic Church sitting together in deep conversation. One wonders what effect the alien visit will have had on these reverend gentlemen. It certainly came as a surprise to many here to find that the White Flame People are intensely religious and also worship a Supreme Being. So far we have learned very little about the form their religion takes.

And now I see that the Prime Minister has arrived with senior members of the Cabinet. The atmosphere is friendly and relaxed. In the centre of the platform are the seats, or should I say couches, which have been specially made for this occasion to give comfort to an alien form that is not quite the same as our human frame.

In every direction, as far as the eye can see, the entire area is tightly packed with spectators, many of them carrying periscopes to obtain a better view. I haven't seen such crowds since the wedding of Prince Charles, our present King, to the lovely Lady Diana those many years back in 1981.

And, talking of Royalty, the Royal entourage of blue liveried hover-cars has just made its appearance at the Park Lane Gate and is making its way slowly up to the platform. Behind it, I can see the White Flame procession equally vivid in its White Flame insignia.

In a respectful hush the Royal Family and the aliens take their places on the platform. All stand silently for a few moments. Many in the crowd have been overcome by tears.

\* \* \*

And now the official speeches by the Prime Minister and the First Lord of the White Flame People are over and it only remains for the aliens to take their personal farewell of the dignitaries on the platform. With great poise they step down from the platform, perhaps about twenty in number and make their solemn way along the red carpet to the awaiting shuttle. At the gleaming entry ports they pause and turn to face the crowds, their arms spread open in a gesture that seems to embrace everyone.

They turn with dignity and step into the craft. The doors silently seal behind them and we have had our last glimpse of the aliens. Almost immediately the shuttle begins to glow softly. It rises slowly for perhaps a hundred metres or so. Now, well clear of the trees, it shines in the sky, rocking back and forth like a pendulum. One final salute from these splendid people. At last it rises vertically at incredible speed and on the instant it is gone; swallowed into the depths of the blue summer sky.

Many in the crowd are weeping as if they had said farewell to a friend. Certainly, a great sense of personal loss is felt here today. I think we all feel it, an emptiness that will be hard to fill. This is Geraldine Bell, in Hyde Park, returning you to the studio.

*Ronald Caie*

63

# AFTERWARDS

In the days and weeks that followed many strange events occurred that were to alter the future of the planet Earth. Although the 'People of the White Flame' had struck a bargain with the British Government they had insisted that this should not prevent them from dealing with other nations. In a short time they were also receiving help from the USA, the USSR and many other countries.

They had also insisted that whatever happened, they would never supply arms or military technology to the nations of the Earth. We know that in the end all went well. The People of the White Flame departed in time to avoid their evil pursuers and the Earth was made safe. At a future time they would return and establish the link between the two planets for the mutual benefit of all their peoples.

In spite of their reservations about the urge of Earth people to use technology for evil purposes they left many wonderful gifts, strange devices such as brilliant ever changing pictures that were constantly varying works of art and wonderful, exotic music that altered in harmony with the moods of the listener. Yet for all their care they did make one mistake. One small object had been left behind, one small machine with a terrible power for good or evil. It had been accidentally dropped in a field somewhere in England. For six months after their departure it had lain undetected until one day it was found. The short play that follows tells the story of what happened then.

# THE FIND

## Scene One

*The playground of St Leonard's Comprehensive. It is the lunchtime break.* DAVID *and* ANGIE *enter walking hand in hand.* MARY *and* ERIC *come running up to them excitedly.*

ERIC: Hello young lovers! Look what we've found up in Tanner's Meadow. (*He holds up a bright metal object that looks like a portable Hi-Fi with a set of headphones attached.*)

ANGIE (*Taking the object from him*): Wow! It's heavy. (*She turns it over examining it.*) That's not a Hi-Fi, there's no place for the cassettes.

DAVE: Maybe it's one of those new laser jobs.

ERIC: Don't be daft. They don't look like that. Besides there's no maker's name or trade mark on it or anything.

MARY: We'd better hand it in. It may be dangerous.

ERIC: You're joking? We might get it to work. You never know what fun we might have with it. (*He puts on the headphones and turns a dial.*) That's funny. I can hear lots of voices all jumbled up. Don't sound like ordinary voices. Spooky like. (*He concentrates for a few moments. The others watch in silence.*) Of course I won't break it, Mary. You're getting to be a right little nag.

MARY: I never said you would. I never said a thing.

ERIC: Yes you did. You said it just now. I heard it clearly through the headphones.

MARY: But it's true, Eric, I didn't say a word.

ERIC: That's rubbish, Dave. What do you mean, it must be a kind of thought-reading machine? They haven't been invented yet.

DAVE: But that's just it. That proves it. I didn't say anything.

ERIC: Yes you did, I heard you clearly.

DAVE: No you didn't. The machine read my thoughts for you. Give me a turn. (*He takes the machine from* ERIC.) Oh Angie! You naughty girl! I can tell what you're thinking just by turning this in your direction.

ANGIE: What was I thinking then?

DAVE (*Laughing*): I don't want to embarrass you in front of the others.

ANGIE: You're kidding. (*She grabs the machine from* DAVE *and puts the headphones on.*) Dave! That's really wicked. You don't really think like that do you?

MARY: But Dave hasn't said a word. Maybe we really can read minds with this machine.

DAVE: We'll have some fun now. Wait till you see!

MARY: Remember it was me that found it. If this machine's what it seems, we'll have to hand it over to the police. You know what it is don't you? It's one of 'theirs'. It's come from 'them'. It's one of those machines they carried around with them attached to their belts and they wouldn't give any explanation when we asked. Remember the one that came to school. He carried a thing like that. Guarded it with his life. It seemed to be the one thing that made them touchy. They must have dropped this one up at Tanner's Meadow that day we had the picnic.

*The bell rings for classes.*

ERIC: Give's it back, Angie. We'll try it out in the class and see what happens. Maybe we'll have some fun!

## Scene Two

*An English classroom at St. Leonard's. The class are already seated noisily getting out their books and folders. Their English teacher,* MR HUGHES, *comes in looking rather weary.*

MR HUGHES (*Automatically*): All right settle down. That's enough of that. Take out your novels and read Chapter Four . . . Silently! (*He slumps down behind his desk and reaches for a pile of papers.*)

ERIC *is sitting next to* DAVE. *He places the headphones on and turns the dial.*

THE DISEMBODIED VOICE OF MR HUGHES: Twenty-three years of marking rubbish like this. Only another thirty-three thousand scripts to mark before I get early retirement – if I'm lucky! Wonder what Janet's got for tea tonight. Tuesday! It's tripe night at the Hughes' again.

*The door opens. The* HEADMASTER *walks in briskly.*

What's the old blighter wanting now?

HEAD: Good afternoon, Mr Hughes. Class busy I see. More silent reading? I must have a word with you later about that. Look Mr Hughes! There's a boy over there wearing a personal Hi-Fi. What next!

THE DISEMBODIED VOICE OF MR HUGHES: Oh Lord! Caught again.

I can't have eyes everywhere. What a busybody pest.

MR HUGHES: Yes headmaster. I'm sorry. It escaped my notice. So much marking to get through. Eric Stewart, bring that out here at once!

ERIC (*Suddenly stands up knocking over his chair*): Got to go now. Sorry. No time to explain. Dental appointment. Bring note tomorrow.

*He rushes out the door past the amazed* HEADMASTER. DAVE *gets up to follow him and then sits down again.*

HEAD: Well this is intolerable! Your discipline is totally unsatisfactory. I'll see you in my office at four o'clock.

*He goes out slamming the door. Class erupts into noise.*

## Scene Three

ERIC*'s parents' sitting room. He is sitting in a corner with the headphones on. His father comes in and sits down on the sofa with the paper.* ERIC *adjusts the dial.*

MR STEWART'S DISEMBODIED VOICE: 'A Liverpool housewife yesterday gave birth to quads. Mother and babies are said to be doing well.' Good God, imagine four kids all growing up at the same time. It must be Hell! (*He looks across at Eric*) One's bad enough. All he does these days is lounge about the house listening to that bloomin' transistor. What a good for nothing. God knows what'll come of it all. If it hadn't been for him I'd have probably left Moira years ago. Could have taken up that job on the rigs – earned big money. To think what I've put up with all these boring years for that thing slouching in the corner plugged into a machine.

ERIC (*Suddenly standing up and yelling*): Dad, that's not fair. You've no right to say those things.

*He rushes out of the room leaving a bewildered* MR STEWART.

MR STEWART: But, I haven't said a thing. (*He scratches his head.*)

## Scene Four

*The High Street on Saturday morning.* ERIC *and* MARY *meet in front of a shop.*

MARY: I see you're still wearing that thing? Have you learned any secrets?

ERIC: Too many. I don't think reading minds is such a great idea after all. Truth's not something we have to know all the time. I've learned a lot these last few days, I can tell you.

MARY: You'll have to hand it over you know, eventually. You can't keep it forever.

ERIC: No fear! I don't want it anymore. I'm going to destroy it, if I can. We're not ready for a machine like this. We can't go on reading each other's minds when we've so many unkind, selfish thoughts knocking about in them all the time. I tell you it's really depressed me this machine.

MARY: Give us a shot.

*As she puts it on a tall sinister looking man stands up beside them, pretending to look into the shop window. He glances at his watch nervously from time to time. MARY adjusts the dial.*

THE DISEMBODIED VOICE OF THE STRANGER (*Nervous and agitated*): Five minutes to rendezvous. I hope Chuck's on time with the van. Better make sure the shooter's O.K. (*He puts a hand into his jacket.*) Safety catch off. God help the blighter that tries to get in my way. Bank job on Saturday. Should clear a few thousand.

MARY *excitedly grips* ERIC *by the arm and looks around quickly. She pulls him towards the bank on the corner of the High Street.*

MARY: That man by the shop's planning a bank raid. He's got a gun. We've got to warn them.

**Scene Five**

*The crowded interior of the bank.* MARY *and* ERIC *rush in through the crowd and push their way to the front.*

MARY (*To the teller behind the counter*): Ring the alarm. The bank's about to be raided. You've only got a few minutes.

TELLER: Now, miss. This is no place for jokes.

MARY: But it's true. I know. I've just heard a man in the street thinking about it. They're coming any minute now.

TELLER: Come on now. You don't expect me to believe that do you?

*The customers laugh.*

ERIC: You'll believe this.

ERIC *snatches the mind reader from* MARY *and smashes it with all his strength against the glass of the teller's kiosk. It disintegrates into hundreds of pieces, at the same time triggering off the alarm. There is a moment's silence then some shouting outside and the sound of police sirens. A few shots are fired.*

## Scene Six

*The sitting room of* ERIC*'s parents' house.* ERIC, MARY *and* MR STEWART *are sitting watching the television news.*

TV: Today an attack on a bank in High Street, Tanner was foiled when the alarm was prematurely triggered by a local schoolboy, Eric Stewart. His friend, Mary Prosser, claimed to have foreknowledge of the raid by the use of an alien thought-reading machine which she had found some days ago in a field outside town. Police arrived promptly on the scene and there were shots exchanged outside the bank. No one was injured but three men are in custody tonight helping police with their enquiries.

As for the alien thought-reading machine, schoolboy Eric claimed that it was smashed to pieces when he used it to fire the alarm system at the bank.

A spokesman for the Ministry of Defence who investigated the scene confirmed that fragments of a machine of alien origin had been found in the bank. They had been collected for analysis. When asked if the machine could be reassembled, he refused to comment.

MR STEWART: Why did you smash the machine Eric? You could easily have set off the alarm another way.

ERIC: If you can't work that one out, Dad, there's no use me telling you.

MR STEWART: You could have a lot of fun with a machine like that. Anyway, that apart, I'm very proud of you and what you did. (*He looks at Mary.*) Both of you. Seems you're not such a layabout after all, Eric.

MRS STEWART *comes in with a loaded tray.*

MRS STEWART: Thought you might all enjoy a treat tonight since you're so famous, heroes and heroines. Scampi and chips all round.

ERIC: Mum! Our favourite! You must be a mind-reader!

# 21

# Exile

I wish now that we hadn't got to talking about science fiction that night! If we hadn't, I wouldn't be haunted now by that queer, impossible story which can't ever be proved or disproved.

But the four of us were all professional writers of fantastic stories, and I suppose shop talk was inevitable. Yet, we'd kept off it through dinner and the drinks afterwards. Madison had outlined his hunting trip with gusto, and then Brazell started a discussion of the Dodgers' chances. And then I had to turn the conversation to fantasy.

I didn't mean to do it. But I'd had an extra Scotch, and that always makes me feel analytical. And I got to feeling amused by the perfect way in which we four resembled a quartet of normal, ordinary people.

'Protective coloration, that's what it is,' I announced. 'How hard we work at the business of acting like ordinary good guys!'

Brazell looked at me, somewhat annoyed by the interruption. 'What are you talking about?'

'About us,' I answered. 'What a wonderful imitation of solid, satisfied citizens we put up! But we're not satisfied, you know – none of us. We're violently dissatisfied with the Earth, and all its works, and that's why we spend our lives dreaming up one imaginary world after another.'

'I suppose the little matter of getting paid for it has nothing to do with it?' Brazell asked sceptically.

'Sure it has,' I admitted. 'But we all dreamed up our impossible worlds and peoples long before we ever wrote a line, didn't we? From back in childhood, even? It's because we don't feel at home here.'

Madison snorted. 'We'd feel a lot less at home on some of the worlds we write about.'

Then Carrick, the fourth of our party, broke into the conversation. He'd been sitting over his drink in his usual silent way, brooding, paying no attention to us.

He was a queer chap, in most ways. We didn't know him very well, but we liked him and admired his stories. He'd done some wonderful tales of an imaginary planet – all carefully worked out.

He told Madison, 'That happened to me.'
'What happened to you?' Madison asked.
'What you were suggesting – *I* once wrote about an imaginary world and then had to live on it,' Carrick answered.
Madison laughed. 'I hope it was a more livable place than the lurid planets on which I set my own yarns.'
But Carrick was unsmiling. He murmured, 'I'd have made it a lot different – if I'd known I was ever going to live on it.'
Brazell, with a significant glance at Carrick's empty glass winked at us and then asked blandly, 'Let's hear about it, Carrick.'


Carrick kept looking dully down at his empty glass, turning it slowly in his fingers as he talked. He paused every few words.
'It happened just after I'd moved next to the big power station. It sounds like a noisy place, but actually it was very quiet out there on the edge of the city. And I had to have quiet, if I was to produce stories.
'I got right to work on a new series I was starting, the stories of which were all to be laid on the same imaginary world. I began by working out the detailed physical appearance of that world, as well as the universe that was its background. I spent the whole day concentrating on that. And, as I finished, something in my mind went *click*!
'That queer, brief mental sensation felt oddly like a sudden *crystallization*. I stood there, wondering if I were going crazy. For I had a sudden strong conviction that it meant that the universe and world I had been dreaming up all day had suddenly crystallized into physical existence somewhere.
'Naturally, I brushed aside the eerie thought and went out and forgot about it. But the next day, the thing happened again. I had spent most of that second day working up the inhabitants of my story world. I'd made them definitely human, but had decided against making them too civilized – for that would exclude the conflict and violence that must form my story.
'So, I'd made my imaginary world a world whose people were still only half-civilized. I figured out all their cruelties and superstitions. I mentally built up their colourful barbaric cities. And just as I was through — that *click*! echoed sharply in my mind.

'It startled me badly, this second time. For now I felt more strongly than before that queer conviction that my day's dreaming had crystallized into solid reality. I knew it was insane to think that, yet it was an incredible certainty in my mind. I couldn't get rid of it.

'I tried to reason the thing out so that I could dismiss that crazy conviction. If my imagining a world and universe had actually created them, where were they? Certainly not in my own cosmos. It couldn't hold two universes – each completely different from the other.

'But maybe that world and universe of my imagining had crystallized into reality in another and empty cosmos? A cosmos lying in a different dimension from my own? One which had contained only free atoms, formless matter that had not taken on shape until my concentrated thought had somehow stirred it into the forms I dreamed?

'I reasoned along like that, in the queer, dreamlike way in which you apply the rules of logic to impossibilities. How did it come that my imaginings had never crystallized into reality before, but had only just begun to do so? Well, there was a plausible explanation for that. It was the big power station nearby. Some unfathomable freak of energy radiated from it was focusing my concentrated imaginings, as super-amplified force, upon an empty cosmos where they stirred formless matter into the shapes I dreamed.

'Did I believe that? No, I didn't believe it – but I knew it. There is quite a difference between knowledge and belief, as someone said who once pointed out that all men know they will die and none of them believe it. It was like that with me. I realized it was not possible that my imaginary world had come into physical being in a different dimensional cosmos, yet at the same time I was strangely convinced that it had.

'A thought occurred to me that amused and interested me. What if I imagined *myself* in that other world? Would I, too, become physically real in it? I tried it. I sat at my desk, imagining myself as one of the millions of persons in that imaginary world, dreaming up a whole soberly realistic background and family and history for myself over there. And my mind said *click!*'

Carrick paused, still looking down at the empty glass that he twirled slowly between his fingers.

Madison prompted him. 'And of course you woke up there, and a beautiful girl was leaning over you, and you asked, "Where am I?"'

'It wasn't like that,' Carrick said dully. 'It wasn't like that at all. I woke up in that other world, yes. But it wasn't like a real awakening. I was just suddenly in it.

'I was still myself. But I was the myself I had imagined in that other world. That other me had always lived in it – and so had his ancestors before him. I had worked all that out, you see.

'And I was just as real to myself, in that imaginary world I had created, as I had been in my own. That was the worst part of it. Everything in that half-civilized world was so utterly, common-placely real.'

He paused again. 'It was queer, at first. I walked out into the streets of those barbaric cities, and looked into the people's faces, and I felt like shouting aloud, "I imagined you all! You had no existence until I dreamed of you!"

'But I didn't do that. They wouldn't have believed me. To them, I was just an insignificant single member of their race. How could they guess that they and their traditions of long history, their world and their universe, had all been suddenly brought into being by my imagination?

'After my first excitement ebbed, I didn't like the place. I had made it too barbaric. The savage violences and cruelties that had seemed so attractive as material for a story, were ugly and repulsive at first hand. I wanted nothing but to get back to my own world.

'And I couldn't get back! There just wasn't any way. I had had a vague idea that I could imagine myself back into my own world as I had imagined myself into this other one. But it didn't work that way. The freak force that had wrought the miracle didn't work two ways.

'I had a pretty bad time when I realized that I was trapped in that ugly, squalid, barbarian world. I felt like killing myself at first. But I didn't. A man can adapt himself to anything. I adapted myself the best I could to the world I had created.'

'What did you do there? What was your position, I mean? Brazell asked.

Carrick shrugged. 'I don't know the crafts or skills of that world I'd brought into being. I had only my own skill – that of story telling.'

I began to grin. 'You don't mean to say that you started writing fantastic stories?'

He nodded soberly. 'I had to. It was all I could do. I wrote stories about my own real world. To those other people my tales were wild imaginations – and they liked them.'

We chuckled. But Carrick was deadly serious.

Madison humoured him to the end. 'And how did you finally get back home from that other world you'd created?'

'I never did get back home,' Carrick said with a heavy sigh.

'Oh, come now,' Madison protested lightly. 'It's obvious that you got back some time.'

Carrick shook his head sombrely as he rose to leave.

'No, I never got back home,' he said soberly. 'I'm still here.'

*Edmond Hamilton*

# 22

# The Future

The Future does not look like this . . .

```
              you
             /are
            / here
PAST       ↙        FUTURE              END
         PRESENT
```

The Future looks more like this . . .

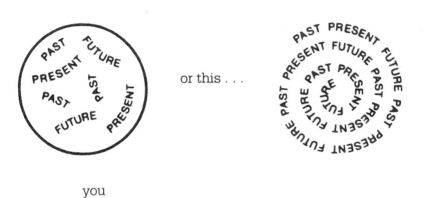

or this . . .

```
        you
        are
or this . . . here
```

*Roger McGough*

# 23

# The Time of His Life

*A dingy single bed-sitting room, very untidy with unwashed clothing and discarded newspapers. In the centre of the room is a small wooden table with the remains of breakfast. To the right is the door to the downstairs hall. At the back is a small window under which is a sink and stand with small gas-burner.*

*When the curtain opens* ALBERT *is discovered placing an egg in a small saucepan.*

ALBERT: Let's see now. Where's the timer? *(He rummages about among the clutter round the sink)* Never mind, I'll use the clock. Drat it's stopped! I'll just have to count up to 3 times 60. That's eh . . . eh . . . roughly 150 seconds. *(There is a loud knock at the door)* That'll be Mrs Snatchit for her rent.

*He tries to do a quick tidy-up and upsets the pan. The egg breaks on the floor in front of the door. There is another loud knock.*

Coming Mrs Snatchit. Just give us a minute. *(He spreads the egg around with his foot and opens the door)*

MRS SNATCHIT: I've come for my rent Mr Smith. It's nearly three weeks since you last paid. Rather too long a time I think.

ALBERT: Goodness is it all that time?

*He goes to the wardrobe left and removes his jacket. He takes out the wallet and after poking around in it for a time turns it inside out with an exasperated gesture.*

Sorry, Mrs Snatchit, I seem to be out of funds just now. Don't get paid till Friday. Only my mother hasn't been very well and I've been sending her a little something from time to time.

MRS SNATCHIT *(advancing into the room)*: I've heard excuses like that before. I wasn't born yesterday, my man.

ALBERT: No, I can see that, Mrs Snatchit. It must've been some time ago.

MRS SNATCHIT: That's enough of that. I'm not going to put up with this much longer. This place is like a pigsty and my patience is at an end. You're running out of time Mr Smith.

ALBERT: I am sorry, Mrs Snatchit. I'll try to clear up and as soon as I get paid you'll get your rent. All I need is a little time.

MRS SNATCHIT: You'll be doing time if you don't pay up soon.

*There is a loud knock on the partly open door and the voice of the* SALESMAN *calls in.*

SALESMAN: Did I hear the word time? Excuse me madam. (*He sidles into the room*) Did I hear you say you wanted time? Now sir, now madam, you've come to the right man. Let me interest you in a little something I'm selling.

MRS SNATCHIT: We allow no salesmen in this building. This is a respectable house. Always has been until recently that is. (*She glares at Albert*)

SALESMAN: I'm sorry missus, I didn't catch the name?

MRS SNATCHIT: Snatchit!

SALESMAN: Snatch what? (*Looks puzzled*)

MRS SNATCHIT (*raising her voice*): Snatchit! Snatchit! That's my name.

SALESMAN (*alarmed by the shouting*): Ah . . . Mrs Snatchit. I see. Well I was just passing, in a manner of speaking, and I happened to hear Mr Snatchit there say that he needed a little time. Now . . .

MRS SNATCHIT (*hurriedly interrupts him*): This man is not my husband! He's Mr Smith.

SALESMAN: Mr Smith? (*A knowing grin and a wink at Mrs Snatchit*) Mr Smith eh? Your secret's all right with me madam. We salesmen are very discreet. (*He touches the side of his nose with his forefinger*)

MRS SNATCHIT: Let me make this perfectly clear. This is my bed-sitting room and Mr Smith lives in it.

SALESMAN: That's all right, madam. No need to spell it out. I'm a man of the world. I've been about a bit.

MRS SNATCHIT: Mr Smith is my lodger. My lodger. Understand? And the reason he needs time is that he is nearly three weeks behind with his rent.

SALESMAN: Ah! . . . Ah! Yes. Well now I may just be able to help him there.

MRS SNATCHIT: Are you a money lender?

SALESMAN: Well no, not quite. But I do have something to sell which I think might help Mr Smith with his rent payments . . . help him to get them to you on time as it were.

ALBERT (*taking an interest for the first time*): Have you now? Why don't you come in properly and sit down?

SALESMAN: Perhaps if Mrs Snatchit wouldn't mind? (*He indicates the door politely*) Just this one time – make an exception to your rule about salesmen. You see it's not an ordinary salesman you're dealing with this time.

MRS SNATCHIT (*looking reluctant*): Well, just this once perhaps. You can have five minutes. Anything would be an improvement with him. But as soon as you're finished you're to leave the building. I don't want any of my other respectable tenants bothered by you. He's different. (*She jabs a thumb at him and sails out with as much dignity as she can muster.*)

ALBERT: Phew! Thank God she's gone. What a dragon! How did you manage it?

SALESMAN: I've had plenty of experience. Always had plenty of time to practise my job properly, always plenty of time – which brings me back to what I heard as I came in. You said you needed time – to pay the rent you owe I suppose?

ALBERT: That's right. You got it in one. Only on my miserable wage I need a lot of time . . . more than till pay day I reckon.

SALESMAN: Now that's where I think I can help you. You see when you say you want time you're thinking about future time aren't you?

ALBERT *nods looking puzzled.*

But what I can offer you as well is *past* time. I can save your wasted time. I can give you literally the time of your life. All those wasted seconds, minutes, hours you thought you'd lost – I can get them back for you.

ALBERT: How? I can't see how.

SALESMAN: I thought you'd ask that, they all do. Can't see. That's just it. You don't have to see. It's all in this small box. (*He takes a small brown box from his pocket and places it on the table.*)

ALBERT (*unimpressed*): What on earth's that?

SALESMAN: It's a time-machine.

ALBERT: A time-machine! There's no such thing. You're a con-man. Anyway, time-machines are big things with flashing lights and dials.

SALESMAN: How do you know that if you say there's no such thing? There are more things in Heaven and Earth, Horatio, than are dreamed of in your philosophy.

ALBERT: The name's Albert. Albert Smith. Not Horatio.

SALESMAN (*giving him a funny look*): It's certainly not Albert Einstein anyway. I was talking figuratively, Albert. I was quoting from Shakespeare's *Hamlet*.

ALBERT: Oh! You see there's not much call for a porter to read Shakespeare. A right bore, I think it is.

SALESMAN: But now that I've mentioned him, Albert Einstein, I can explain a little about this time-machine. You've no doubt heard of his famous theory of relativity?

ALBERT: Can't say I have. He was the man that invented the atom bomb. Too clever by half if you ask me.

SALESMAN: Not quite. Not quite like that Albert. It was Einstein who first showed us that time is relative to speed. You see, if you left Earth in 1984 in a spaceship travelling very near the speed of light, and you made a long voyage

taking perhaps 8 years, you wouldn't come back in 1992, you'd come back in the 2020s. All your friends and relations, your wife perhaps, even a twin brother would all be very much older than you. That's because time is relative to the speed you're travelling.

ALBERT: That's nonsense.

SALESMAN: No it's not. And this little time-machine can prove it.

ALBERT: I'm not parting with any money for that thing until I see what it can do.

SALESMAN: No need. (*He picks it up and demonstrates it to* ALBERT.) You see this dial here like the face of a clock? You set the hands to the point you wish to go back to, then all you do is press the button and whoosh, you're back. You can have your time over again, even make a few changes if you wish. Or simply set the hands forward and come zooming back to the old present again. On the other side is a calendar with days, weeks, months, years, centuries, etc. You set it the same way and press the button. What ever you do, never travel back less than an hour in time. That could be very dangerous.

ALBERT: But how can that help me to pay the rent on time?

SALESMAN (*exasperated*): All you have to do once you have the money is dial yourself back to the time when it was first due, pay it promptly to Mrs Snatchit, then bring yourself back to the present. Her memory will have changed meanwhile and your rent book will be up-to-date. And just think what you could get out of the horses!

ALBERT: What's horses got to do with it?

SALESMAN: I'll explain when I come back tomorrow. I'm going to give you a 24-hour free trial with the machine. No obligation if you don't like it.

ALBERT: But if it really does do what you say it does I reckon'll it'll be expensive. How much?

SALESMAN: Only 2 million pounds, cash down. You pay it up on the never-never. That's a good one. Never-never! (*He laughs loudly at* ALBERT'*s puzzled face.*) After the down-payment you pay a million a month for as long as it takes.

ALBERT: I'll never afford that. That's impossible.

SALESMAN: With this machine nothing is impossible.

ALBERT: What if I steal it?

SALESMAN: You can't. We've ways of tracking it down. All you have to do is use your imagination and your intelligence. You'll have a great time. But remember, never use it for going back less than one hour. That's the only danger. That and getting eaten by a dinosaur!

ALBERT: A dinosaur?

SALESMAN: Oh never mind. (*He gets up suddenly and makes for the door.*) Remember I'll be back tomorrow same time. Oh! Your clock's stopped. I hope that's not a bad omen! Ha! Ha!

*He goes out slamming the door behind him but he has left his hat on the table.*

ALBERT (*sits puzzling at the machine in front of him, scarcely daring to touch it*): Funny sort of bloke. Practical joke I shouldn't be surprised. Oh, look at that. He's forgotten his hat. (*He thinks for a bit*) I know what I can do. If it works, I'll set it back for a few minutes to when he walked out and then I can give his hat back.

*He fiddles briefly with the clock dial on the machine. Then presses the button. There is a loud bang and a flash of light. ALBERT is still seated at the table as before.*

Funny sort of bloke. Practical joke I shouldn't be surprised. Oh, look at that. He's forgotten his hat. I know what I can do. If it works, I'll set it back for a few minutes to when he walked out and then I can give his hat back.

*He fiddles briefly with the clock dial on the machine. Then presses the button. There is a loud bang and a flash of light. ALBERT is still seated at the table as before.*

Funny sort of bloke . . .

*There is another bang and flash and the SALESMAN suddenly appears standing next to ALBERT who seems to be unaware of his presence. He is still saying the same words over and over again. The SALESMAN nods his head sadly, picks up the time-machine and places his forgotten hat on his head.*

SALESMAN: Some of them never learn. Poor Albert. I guess we might say, 'He's having the time of his life.' One thing's sure, Mrs Snatchit'll never get her rent now. There'll just never be enough time.

*Ronald Caie*

# 24

# Harrison Bergeron

The year was 2081, and everybody was finally equal. They weren't only equal before God and the law, they were equal every which way. Nobody was smarter than anybody else; nobody was better looking than anybody else; nobody was stronger or quicker than anybody else. All this equality was due to the 211th, 212th, and 213th Amendments to the Constitution, and to the unceasing vigilance of agents of the United States Handicapper General.

It was tragic, all right, but George and Hazel couldn't think about it very hard. Hazel had a perfectly average intelligence, which meant she couldn't think about anything except in short bursts. And George, while his intelligence was way above normal, had a little mental handicap radio in his ear – he was required by law to wear it at all times. It was tuned to a government transmitter, and every twenty seconds or so the transmitter would send out some sharp noise to keep people like George from taking unfair advantage of their brains.

George and Hazel were watching television. There were tears on Hazel's cheeks, but she'd forgotten for the moment what they were about, as the ballerinas came to the end of a dance.

A buzzer sounded in George's head. His thoughts fled in panic, like bandits from a burglar alarm.

'That was a real pretty dance, that dance they just did,' said Hazel.

'Huh?' said George.

'That dance – it was nice,' said Hazel.

'That was a real pretty dance, that dance they just did,' said Hazel.

'Huh?' said George.

'That dance – it was nice,' said Hazel.

'Yup,' said George. He tried to think a little about the ballerinas. They weren't really very good – no better than anybody else would have been, anyway. They were burdened with sash-weights and bags of birdshot, and their faces were masked, so that no one, seeing a free and graceful gesture or a pretty face, would feel like something the cat dragged in. George was toying with the vague notion that maybe dancers shouldn't be handicapped. But he didn't get very far with it before another noise in his ear radio scattered his thoughts.

George winced. So did two out of the eight ballerinas. Hazel saw him wince. Having no mental handicap herself, she had to ask George what the latest sound had been.

'Sounded like somebody hitting a milk bottle with a ball-peen hammer,' said George.

'I'd think it would be real interesting, hearing all the different sounds,' said Hazel, a little envious. 'The things they think up.'

'Um,' said George.

'Only, if I was Handicapper General, you know what I would do?' said Hazel. Hazel, as a matter of fact, bore a strong resemblance to the Handicapper General, a woman named Diana Moon Glampers. 'If I was Diana Moon Glampers,' said Hazel, 'I'd have chimes on Sunday – just chimes. Kind of in honour of religion.'

'I could think, if it was just chimes,' said George.

'Well – maybe make 'em real loud,' said Hazel. 'I think I'd make a good Handicapper General.'

'Good as anybody else,' said George.

'Who knows better'n I do what normal is?' said Hazel.

'Right,' said George. He began to think glimmeringly about his abnormal son who was now in jail, about Harrison, but a twenty-one gun salute in his head stopped that.

'Boy!' said Hazel, 'that was a doozy, wasn't it?'

It was such a doozy that George was white and trembling, and tears stood on the rims of his red eyes. Two of the eight ballerinas had collapsed to the studio floor, were holding their temples.

'All of a sudden you look so tired,' said Hazel. 'Why don't you stretch out on the sofa, so's you can rest your handicap bag on the pillows, honeybunch?' She was referring to the forty-seven pounds of birdshot in a canvas bag, which was padlocked around George's neck. 'Go on and rest the bag for a little while,' she said. 'I don't care if you're not equal to me for a while.'

George weighed the bag with his hands. 'I don't mind it,' he said. 'I don't notice it any more. It's just a part of me.'

'You've been so tired lately – kind of wore out,' said Hazel. 'If there was just some way we could make a little hole in the bottom of the bag, and just take out a few of them lead balls.

Just a few.'

'Two years in prison and two thousand dollars fine for every ball I took out,' said George. 'I don't call that a bargain.'

'If you could just take a few out when you come home from work,' said Hazel. 'I mean – you don't compete with anybody around here. You just set around.'

'If I tried to get away with it,' said George, 'then other people'd get away with it – and pretty soon we'd be right back to the dark ages again, with everybody competing against everybody else. You wouldn't like that, would you?'

'I'd hate it,' said Hazel.

'There you are,' said George. 'The minute people start cheating on laws, what do you think happens to society?'

If Hazel hadn't been able to come up with an answer to this question, George couldn't have supplied one. A siren was going off in his head.

'Reckon it'd fall all apart,' said Hazel.

'What would?' said George blankly.

'Society,' said Hazel uncertainly. 'Wasn't that what you just said?'

'Who knows?' said George.

The television programme was suddenly interrupted for a news bulletin. It wasn't clear at first as to what the bulletin was about, since the announcer, like all announcers, had a serious speech impediment. For about half a minute, and in a state of high excitement, the announcer tried to say, 'Ladies and gentlemen –'

He finally gave up, handed the bulletin to a ballerina to read.

'That's all right,' Hazel said of the announcer, 'he tried. That's the big thing. He tried to do the best he could with what God gave him. He should get a nice raise for trying so hard.'

'Ladies and gentlemen –' said the ballerina, reading the bulletin. She must have been extraordinarily beautiful, because the mask she wore was hideous. And it was easy to see that she was the strongest and most graceful of all the dancers, for her handicap bags were as big as those worn by two-hundred-pound men.

And she had to apologize at once for her voice, which was a very unfair voice for a woman to use. Her voice was a warm, luminous, timeless melody. 'Excuse me –' she said, and she began again, making her voice absolutely un-competitive.

'Harrison Bergeron, age fourteen,' she said in a grackle squawk, 'has just escaped from jail, where he was held on suspicion of plotting to overthrow the government. He is a genius and an athlete, is under-handicapped, and is extremely dangerous.'

A police photograph of Harrison Bergeron was flashed on the screen – upside down, then sideways, upside down again, then right-side up. The picture showed the full length of Harrison against a background calibrated in feet and inches. He was exactly seven feet tall.

The rest of Harrison's appearance was Halloween and hardware. Nobody had ever borne heavier handicaps. He had outgrown hindrances faster than the H-G men could think them up. Instead of a little ear radio for a mental handicap, he wore a tremendous pair of earphones, and spectacles with thick, wavy lenses besides. The spectacles were intended not only to make him half blind, but to give him whanging headaches besides.

Scrap metal was hung all over him. Ordinarily, there was a certain symmetry, a military neatness to the handicaps issued to strong people, but Harrison looked like a walking junkyard. In the race of life Harrison carried three hundred pounds.

And to offset his good looks, the H-G men required that he wear at all times a red rubber ball for a nose, keep his eyebrows shaved off, and cover his even white teeth with black caps at snaggle-tooth random.

'If you see this boy,' said the ballerina, 'do not – I repeat, do not – try to reason with him.'

There was the shriek of a door being torn from its hinges.

Screams and barking cries of consternation came from the television set. The photograph of Harrison Bergeron on the screen jumped again and again, as though dancing to the tune of an earthquake.

George Bergeron correctly identified the earthquake, and well he might have – for many was the time his own home had danced to the same crashing tune. 'My God!' said George. 'That must be Harrison!'

The realization was blasted from his mind instantly by the sound of an automobile collision in his head.

When George could open his eyes again, the photograph of Harrison was gone. A living, breathing Harrison filled the screen.

Clanking, clownish, and huge, Harrison stood in the centre of the studio. The knob of the uprooted studio door was still in his hand. Ballerinas, technicians, musicians and announcers cowered on their knees before him, expecting to die.

'I am the Emperor!' cried Harrison. 'Do you hear? I am the Emperor! Everybody must do what I say at once!' He stamped his foot and the studio shook.

'Even as I stand here,' he bellowed, 'cripped, hobbled, sickened – I am a greater ruler than any man who ever lived! Now watch me become what I *can* become!'

Harrison tore the straps of his handicap harness like wet tissue paper, tore straps guaranteed to support five thousand pounds.

Harrison's scrap-iron handicaps crashed to the floor.

Harrison thrust his thumbs under the bar of the padlock that secured his head harness. The bar snapped like celery. Harrison smashed his headphones and spectacles against the wall.

He flung away his rubber-ball nose, revealed a man that would have awed Thor, the god of thunder.

'I shall now select my Empress!' he said, looking down on the cowering people. 'Let the first woman who dares rise to

her feet claim her mate and her throne!'

A moment passed, and then a ballerina arose, swaying like a willow.

Harrison plucked the mental handicap from her ear, snapped off her physical handicaps with marvellous delicacy. last of all, he removed her mask.

She was blindingly beautiful.

'Now –' said Harrison, taking her hand. 'Shall we show the people the meaning of the word dance? Music!' he commanded.

The musicians scrambled back into their chairs, and Harrison stripped them of their handicaps, too. 'Play your best,' he told them, 'and I'll make you barons and dukes and earls.'

The music began. It was normal at first – cheap, silly, false. But Harrison snatched two musicians from their chairs, waved them like batons as he sang the music as he wanted it played. He slammed them back into their chairs.

The music began again, and was much improved.

Harrison and his Empress merely listened to the music for a while – listened gravely, as though synchronizing their heartbeats with it.

They shifted their weight to their toes.

Harrison placed his big hands on the girl's tiny waist, letting her sense the weightlessness that would soon be hers.

And then, in an explosion of joy and grace, into the air they sprang!

Not only were the laws of the land abandoned, but the law of gravity and the laws of motion as well.

They reeled, whirled, swivelled, flounced, capered, gambolled and spun.

They leaped like deer on the moon.

The studio ceiling was thirty feet high, but each leap brought the dancers nearer to it.

It became their obvious intention to kiss the ceiling.

They kissed it.

And then, neutralizing gravity with love and pure will, they remained suspended in air inches below the ceiling, and they kissed each other for a long, long time.

It was then that Diana Moon Glampers, the Handicapper General, came into the studio with a double-barrelled ten-gauge shot-gun. She fired twice, and the Emperor and the Empress were dead before they hit the floor.

Diana Moon Glampers loaded the gun again. She aimed it at the musicians and told them they had ten seconds to get their handicaps back on.

It was then that the Bergerons' television tube burned out.

Hazel turned to comment about the blackout to George. But George had gone out into the kitchen for a can of beer.

George came back in with the beer, paused while a handicap signal shook him up. And then he sat down again. 'You been crying?' he said to Hazel, watching her wipe her tears.

'Yup,' she said.

'What about?' he said.

'I forget,' she said. 'Something real sad on television.'

'What was it?' he said.

'It's all kind of mixed up in my mind,' said Hazel.

'Forget sad things,' said George.

'I always do,' said Hazel.

'That's my girl,' said George. He winced. There was the sound of a rivetting gun in his head.

'Gee – I could tell that one was a doozy,' said Hazel.

'You can say that again,' said George.

'Gee –' said Hazel – 'I could tell that one was a doozy.'

*Kurt Vonnegut*

# 25

# Examination Day

The Jordans never spoke of the exam, not until their son, Dickie, was twelve years old. It was on his birthday that Mrs Jordan first mentioned the subject in his presence, and the anxious manner of her speech caused her husband to answer sharply.

'Forget about it,' he said. 'He'll do all right.'

They were at the breakfast table, and the boy looked up from his plate curiously. He was an alert-eyed youngster, with flat blond hair and a quick, nervous manner. He didn't understand what the sudden tension was about, but he did know that today was his birthday, and he wanted harmony above all. Somewhere in the little apartment there were wrapped, beribboned packages waiting to be opened, and in the tiny wall-kitchen, something warm and sweet was being prepared in the automatic stove. He wanted the day to be happy, and the moistness of his mother's eyes, the scowl on his father's face, spoiled the mood of fluttering expectation with which he had greeted the morning.

'What exam?' he asked.

His mother looked at the tablecloth. 'It's just a sort of Government intelligence test they give children at the age of twelve. You'll be getting it next week. It's nothing to worry about.'

'You mean a test like in school?'

'Something like that,' his father said, getting up from the table. 'Go read your comic books, Dickie.'

The boy rose and wandered towards that part of the living room which had been 'his' corner since infancy. He fingered the topmost comic of the stack, but seemed uninterested in the colorful squares of fast-paced action. He wandered towards the window, and peered gloomily at the veil of mist that shrouded the glass.

'Why did it have to rain *today*?' he said. 'Why couldn't it rain tomorrow?'

His father, now slumped into an armchair with the Government newspaper, rattled the sheets in vexation. 'Because it just did, that's all. Rain makes the grass grow.'

'Why, Dad?'

'Because it does, that's all.'

Dickie puckered his brow. 'What makes it green, though? The grass?'

'Nobody knows,' his father snapped, then immediately regretted his abruptness.

Later in the day, it was birthday time again. His mother beamed as she handed over the gaily-coloured packages, and even his father managed a grin and a rumple-of-the-hair. He kissed his mother and shook hands gravely with his father. Then the birthday cake was brought forth, and the ceremonies concluded.

An hour later, seated by the window, he watched the sun force its way between the clouds.

'Dad,' he said, 'how far away is the sun?'

'Five thousand miles,' his father said.


Dick sat at the breakfast table and again saw moisture in his mother's eyes. He didn't connect her tears with the exam until his father suddenly brought the subject to light again.

'Well, Dickie,' he said, with a manly frown, 'you've got an appointment today.'

'I know, Dad. I hope –'

'Now it's nothing to worry about. Thousands of children take this test every day. The Government wants to know how smart you are, Dickie. That's all there is to it.'

'I get good marks in school,' he said hesitantly.

'This is different. This is a – special kind of test. They give you this stuff to drink, you see, and then you go into a room where there's a sort of machine –'

'What stuff to drink?' Dickie said.

'It's nothing. It tastes like peppermint. It's just to make sure you answer the questions truthfully. Not that the Government thinks you won't tell the truth, but this stuff makes *sure*.'

Dickie's face showed puzzlement, and touch of fright. He looked at his mother, and she composed her face into a misty smile.

'Everything will be all right,' she said.

'Of course it will,' his father agreed. 'You're a good boy, Dickie; you'll make out fine. Then we'll come home and celebrate. All right?'

'Yes, sir,' Dickie said.

They entered the Government Educational Building fifteen minutes before the appointed hour. They crossed the marble floors of the great pillared lobby, passed beneath an archway and entered an automatic elevator that brought them to the fourth floor.

There was a young man wearing an insignia-less tunic, seated at a polished desk in front of Room 404. He held a clipboard in his hand, and he checked the list down to the Js and permitted the Jordans to enter.

The room was as cold and official as a courtroom, with long benches flanking metal tables. There were several fathers and sons already there, and a thin-lipped woman with cropped black hair was passing out sheets of paper.

Mr Jordan filled out the form, and returned it to the clerk. Then he told Dickie: 'It won't be long now. When they call your name, you just go through the doorway at that end of the room.' He indicated the portal with his finger.

A concealed loudspeaker crackled and called off the first name. Dickie saw a boy leave his father's side reluctantly and walk slowly towards the door.

At five minutes of eleven, they called the name of Jordan.

'Good luck, son,' his father said, without looking at him. 'I'll call for you when the test is over.'

Dickie walked to the door and turned the knob. The room inside was dim, and he could barely make out the features of the gray-tunicked attendant who greeted him.

'Sit down,' the man said softly. He indicated a high stool beside his desk. 'Your name's Richard Jordan?'

'Yes, sir.'

'Your classification number is 600-115. Drink this, Richard.'

He lifted a plastic cup from the desk and handed it to the boy. The liquid inside had the consistency of buttermilk, tasted only vaguely of the promised peppermint. Dickie downed it, and handed the man the empty cup.

He sat in silence, feeling drowsy, while the man wrote busily on a sheet of paper. Then the attendant looked at his watch, and rose to stand only inches from Dickie's face. He unclipped a pen-like object from the pocket of his tunic, and flashed a tiny light into the boy's eyes.

'All right,' he said. 'Come with me, Richard.'

He led Dickie to the end of the room, where a single wooden armchair faced a multi-dialled computing machine. There was a microphone on the left arm of the chair, and when the boy sat down, he found its pinpoint head conveniently at his mouth.

'Now just relax, Richard. You'll be asked some questions, and you think them over carefully. Then give your answers into the microphone. The machine will take care of the rest.'

'Yes, sir.'

'I'll leave you alone now. Whenever you want to start, just say "ready" into the microphone.'

'Yes, sir.'

The man squeezed his shoulder, and left.

Dickie said, 'Ready.'

Lights appeared on the machine, and a mechanism whirred. A voice said:

'Complete this sequence. One, four,seven, ten . . .'

Mr and Mrs Jordan were in the living room, not speaking, not even speculating.

It was almost four o'clock when the telephone rang. The woman tried to reach it first, but her husband was quicker.

'Mr Jordan?'

The voice was clipped; a brisk, official voice.

'Yes, speaking.'

'This is the Government Educational Service. Your son, Richard M Jordan, Classification 600-115, has completed the Government examination. We regret to inform you that his intelligence quotient has exceeded the Government regulation, according to Rule 84, Section 5, of the New Code.'

Across the room, the woman cried out, knowing nothing except the emotion she read on her husband's face.

'You may specify by telephone,' the voice droned on, 'whether you wish his body interred by the Government or would you prefer a private burial place? The fee for Government burial is ten dollars.'

*Henry Slesar*

# 26

# The Store of the Worlds

Mr Wayne came to the end of the long, shoulder-high mound of grey rubble, and there was the Store of the Worlds. It was exactly as his friends had described; a small shack constructed of bits of lumber, parts of cars, a piece of galvanised iron and a few rows of crumbling bricks, all daubed over with a watery blue paint.

Mr Wayne glanced back down the long lane of rubble to make sure he hadn't been followed. He tucked his parcel more firmly under his arm; then, with a little shiver at his own audacity, he opened the door and slipped inside.

'Good morning,' the proprietor said.

He, too, was exactly as described; a tall, crafty-looking old fellow with narrow eyes and a downcast mouth. His name was Tompkins. He sat in an old rocking-chair, and perched on the back of it was a blue and green parrot. There was one other chair in the store, and a table. On the table was a rusted hypodermic.

'I've heard about your store from friends,' Mr Wayne said.

'Then you know my price,' Tompkins said. 'Have you brought it?'

'Yes,' said Mr Wayne, holding up his parcel, 'but I want to ask first —'

'They always want to ask,' Tompkins said to the parrot, who blinked. 'Go ahead, ask.'

'I want to know what really happens.'

Tompkins sighed. 'What happens is this. You pay me my fee. I give you an injection which knocks you out. Then, with the aid of certain gadgets which I have in the back of the store, I liberate your mind.'

Tompkins smiled as he said that, and his silent parrot seemed to smile too.

'What happens then?' Mr Wayne asked.

'Your mind, liberated from its body, is able to choose from the countless probability-worlds which the Earth casts off in every second of its existence.'

Grinning now, Tompkins sat up in his rocking-chair and began to show signs of enthusiasm.

'Yes, my friend, though you might not have suspected it,

from the moment this battered Earth was born out of the sun's fiery womb, it cast off its alternate-probability worlds. Worlds without end, emanating from events large and small; every Alexander and every amoeba creating worlds, just as ripples will spread in a pond no matter how big or how small the stone you throw. Doesn't every object cast a shadow? Well, my friend, the Earth itself is four-dimensional; therefore it casts three-dimensional shadows, solid reflections of itself through every moment of its being. Millions, billions of Earths! An infinity of Earths! And your mind, liberated by me, will be able to select any of these worlds, and to live upon it for a while.'

Mr Wayne was uncomfortably aware that Tompkins sounded like a circus barker, proclaiming marvels that simply couldn't exist. But, Mr Wayne reminded himself, things had happened within his own lifetime which he would never have believed possible. Never! So perhaps the wonders that Tompkins spoke of were possible, too.

Mr Wayne said, 'My friends also told me –'

'That I was an out-and-out fraud?' Tompkins asked.

'Some of them *implied* that,' Mr Wayne said cautiously. 'But I try to keep an open mind. They also said –'

'I know what your dirty-minded friends said. They told you about the fulfilment of desire. Is that what you want to hear about?'

'Yes,' said Mr Wayne. 'They told me that whatever I wished for – whatever I wanted –'

'Exactly,' Tompkins said. 'The thing could work in no other way. There are the infinite worlds to choose among. Your mind chooses, and is guided only by desire. Your deepest desire is the only thing that counts. If you have been harbouring a secret dream of murder –'

'Oh, hardly, hardly!' cried Mr Wayne.

'– then you will go to a world where you *can* murder, where you can roll in blood, where you can outdo Sade or Caesar, or whoever your idol may be. Suppose it's power you want? Then you'll choose a world where you are a god, literally and actually. A blood-thirsty Juggernaut, perhaps, or an all-wise Buddha.'

'I doubt very much if I –'

'There are other desires, too,' Tompkins said. 'All heavens and all hells. Unbridled sexuality. Gluttony, drunkenness, love, fame – anything you want.'

'Amazing!' said Mr Wayne.

'Yes,' Tompkins agreed. 'Of course, my little list doesn't exhaust all the possibilities, all the combinations and permutations of desire. For all I know you might want a simple, placid, pastoral existence on a South Seas island among idealised natives.'

'That sounds more like me,' Mr Wayne said, with a shy laugh.

'But who knows?' Tompkins asked. 'Even you might not know what your true desires are. They might involve your own death.'

'Does that happen often?' Mr Wayne asked anxiously.

'Occasionally.'

'I wouldn't want to die,' Mr Wayne said.

'It hardly ever happens,' Tompkins said, looking at the parcel in Mr Wayne's hands.

'If you say so . . . But how do I know all this is real? Your fee is extremely high, it'll take everything I own. And for all I know, you'll give me a drug and I'll just *dream*! Everything I own just for a – a shot of heroin and a lot of fancy words!'

Tompkins smiled reassuringly. 'The experience has no drug-like quality about it. And no sensation of a dream, either.'

'If it's *true*,' Mr Wayne said, a little petulantly, 'why can't I stay in the world of my desire for good?'

'I'm working on that,' Tompkins said. 'That's why I charge so high a fee; to get materials, to experiment. I'm trying to find a way of making the transition permanent. So far I haven't been able to loosen the cord that binds a man to his own Earth – and pulls him back to it. Not even the great mystics could cut that cord, except with death. But I still have my hopes.'

'It would be a great thing if you succeeded,' Mr Wayne said politely.

'Yes it would!' Tompkins cried, with a surprising burst of passion. 'For then I'd turn my wretched shop into an escape hatch! My process would be free then, free for everyone! Everyone would go to the Earth of their desires, the Earth that really suited them, and leave *this* damned place to the rats and worms –'

Tompkins cut himself off in mid-sentence, and became icy calm. 'But I fear my prejudices are showing. I can't offer a permanent escape from the Earth yet; not one that doesn't involve death. Perhaps I never will be able to. For now, all I can offer you is a vacation, a change, a taste of another world and a look at your own desires. You know my fee. I'll refund it if the experience isn't satisfactory.'

'That's good of you,' Mr Wayne said, quite earnestly. 'But there's the other matter my friends told me about. The ten years off my life.'

'That can't be helped,' Tompkins said, 'and can't be refunded. My process is a tremendous strain on the nervous system, and life-expectancy is shortened accordingly. That's one of the reasons why our so-called government has declared my process illegal.'

'But they don't enforce the ban very firmly,' Mr Wayne said.

'No. Officially the process is banned as a harmful fraud. But officials are men, too. They'd like to leave this Earth, just like everyone else.'

'The cost,' Mr Wayne mused, gripping his parcel tightly. 'And ten years off my life! For the fulfilment of my secret desires . . . Really, I must give this some thought.'

'Think away,' Tompkins said indifferently.

All the way home Mr Wayne thought about it. When his train reached Port Washington, Long Island, he was still thinking. And driving his car from the station to his home he was still thinking about Tompkins's crafty old face, and worlds of probability, and the fulfilment of desire.

But when he stepped inside his house, those thoughts had to stop. Janet, his wife, wanted him to speak sharply to the maid, who had been drinking again. His son Tommy wanted help with the sloop, which was to be launched tomorrow. And his baby daughter wanted to tell about her day in kindergarten.

Mr Wayne spoke pleasantly but firmly to the maid. He helped Tommy put the final coat of copper paint on the sloop's bottom, and he listened to Peggy tell about her adventures in the playground.

Later, when the children were in bed and he and Janet were alone in their living-room, she asked him if something were wrong.

'Wrong?'

'You seem to be worried about something,' Janet said. 'Did you have a bad day at the office?'

'Oh, just the usual sort of thing . . .'

He certainly was not going to tell Janet, or anyone else, that he had taken the day off and gone to see Tompkins in his crazy old Store of the Worlds. Nor was he going to speak about the right every man should have, once in his lifetime, to fulfil his most secret desires. Janet, with her good common sense, would never understand that.

The next days at the office were extremely hectic. All of Wall Street was in a mild panic over events in the Middle East and in Asia, and stocks were reacting accordingly. Mr Wayne settled down to work. He tried not to think of the fulfilment of desire at the cost of everything he possessed, with ten years of his life thrown in for good measure. It was crazy! Old Tompkins must be insane!

On week-ends he went sailing with Tommy. The old sloop was behaving very well, making practically no water through her bottom seams. Tommy wanted a new suit of racing sails, but Mr Wayne sternly rejected that. Perhaps next year, if the market looked better. For now, the old sails would have to do.

Sometimes at night, after the children were asleep, he and Janet would go sailing. Long Island Sound was quiet then, and cool. Their boat glided past the blinking buoys, sailing towards the swollen yellow moon.

'I *know* something's on your mind,' Janet said.

'Darling, please!'

'Is there something you're keeping from me?'

'Nothing!'

'Are you sure? Are you absolutely sure?'

'Absolutely sure.'

'Then put your arms around me. That's right . . .'

And the sloop sailed itself for a while.


Desire and fulfilment . . . But autumn came, and the sloop had to be hauled. The stock market regained some stability, but Peggy caught the measles. Tommy wanted to know the differences between ordinary bombs, atom bombs, hydrogen bombs, cobalt bombs, and all the other kinds of bombs that were in the news. Mr Wayne explained to the best of his ability. And the maid quit unexpectedly.

Secret desires were all very well. Perhaps he *did* want to kill someone, or live on a South Seas island. But there were responsibilities to consider. He had two growing children, and a better wife than he deserved.

Perhaps around Christmas time . . .

But in mid-winter there was a fire in the unoccupied guest bedroom due to defective wiring. The firemen put out the blaze without much damage, and no one was hurt. But it put any thought of Tompkins out of his mind for a while. First the bedroom had to be repaired, for Mr Wayne was very proud of his gracious old house.

Business was still frantic and uncertain due to the international situation. Those Russians, those Arabs, those Greeks, those Chinese. The intercontinental missiles, the atom bombs, the sputniks . . . Mr Wayne spent long days at the office, and sometimes evenings, too. Tommy caught the mumps. A part of the roof had to be re-shingled. And then already it was time to consider the spring launching of the sloop.

A year had passed, and he'd had very little time to think of secret desires. But perhaps next year. In the meantime –


'Well?' said Tompkins. 'Are you all right?'

'Yes, quite all right,' Mr Wayne said. He got up from the chair and rubbed his forehead.

'Do you want a refund?' Tompkins asked.

'No. The experience was quite satisfactory.'

'They always are,' Tompkins said, winking lewdly at the parrot. 'Well, what was yours?'

'A world of the recent past,' Mr Wayne said.

'A lot of them are. Did you find out about your secret desire? Was it murder? Or a South Seas island?'

'I'd rather not discuss it,' Mr Wayne said, pleasantly but firmly.

'A lot of people won't discuss it with me,' Tompkins said sulkily. 'I'll be damned if I know why.'

'Because – well, I think the world of one's secret desire feels sacred, somehow. No offence . . . Do you think you'll ever be able to make it permanent? The world of one's choice, I mean?'

The old man shrugged his shoulders. 'I'm trying. If I succeed, you'll hear about it. Everyone will.'

'Yes, I suppose so.' Mr Wayne undid his parcel and laid its contents on the table. The parcel contained a pair of army boots, a knife, two coils of copper wire, and three small cans of corned beef.

Tompkins's eyes glittered for a moment. 'Quite satisfactory,' he said. 'Thank you.'

'Good-bye,' said Mr Wayne. 'And thank *you*.'


Mr Wayne left the shop and hurried down to the end of the lane of grey rubble. Beyond it, as far as he could see, lay flat fields of rubble, brown and grey and black. Those fields, stretching to every horizon, were made of the twisted corpses of cities, the shattered remnants of trees, and the fine white ash that once was human flesh and bone.

'Well,' Mr Wayne said to himself, 'at least we gave as good as we got.'

That year in the past had cost him everything he owned, and ten years of life thrown in for good measure. Had it been a dream? It was still worth it! But now he had to put away all thought of Janet and the children. That was finished, unless Tompkins perfected his process. Now he had to think about his own survival.

With the aid of his wrist geiger he found a deactivated lane through the rubble. He'd better get back to the shelter before dark, before the rats came out. If he didn't hurry he'd miss the evening potato ration.

*Robert Sheckley*

# 27

# Saturn

Packing my bags – going away
To a place where the air is clean
On Saturn
There's no sense to sit and watch people die
We don't fight our wars the way you do
We put back all the things we use
On Saturn
There's no sense to keep on doing such crimes

There's no principles in what you say
No direction in the things you do
For your world is soon to come to a close
Through the ages all great men have taught
Truth and happiness just can't be bought – or sold
Tell me why are you people so cold

I'm . . .
Going back to Saturn where the rings all glow
Rainbow, moonbeams and orange snow
On Saturn
People live to be two hundred and five
Going back to Saturn where the people smile

Don't need cars 'cause we've learned to fly
On Saturn
Just to live to us is our natural high
We have come here many times before
To find your strategy to peace is war
Killing helpless men, women and children
That don't even know what they're dying for
We can't trust you when you take a stand
With a gun and bible in your hand
And the cold expression on your face
Saying give us what we want or we'll destroy the human race

I'm . . .
Going back to Saturn where the rings all glow
Rainbow, moonbeams and orange snow
On Saturn
People live to be two hundred and five
Going back to Saturn where the people smile
Don't need cars cause we've learned to fly
On Saturn
Just to live to us is our natural high

*Stevie Wonder and Mike Sembello*

# 28

# The Smile

In the town square the queue had formed at five in the morning, while cocks were crowing far out in the rimed country and there were no fires. All about, among the ruined buildings, bits of mist had clung at first, but now with the new light of seven o'clock it was beginning to disperse. Down the road, in twos and threes, more people were gathering in for the day of marketing, the day of festival.

The small boy stood immediately behind two men who had been talking loudly in the clear air, and all of the sounds they made seemed twice as loud because of the cold. The small boy stamped his feet and blew on his red, chapped hands, and looked up at the soiled gunny-sack clothing of the men, and down the long line of men and women ahead.

'Here boy, what're you doing out so early?' said the man behind him.

'Got my place in line, I have,' said the boy.

'Whyn't you run off, give your place to someone who appreciates?'

'Leave the boy alone,' said the man ahead, suddenly turning.

'I was joking.' The man behind put his hand on the boy's head. The boy shook it away coldly. 'I just thought it strange, a boy out of bed so early.'

'This boy's an appreciator of arts, I'll have you know,' said the boy's defender, a man named Grisby. 'What's your name, lad?'

'Tom.'

'Tom here is going to spit clean and true, right, Tom?'

'I sure am!'

Laughter passed down the line.

A man was selling cracked cups of hot coffee up ahead. Tom looked and saw the little hot fire and the brew bubbling in a rusty pan. It wasn't really coffee. It was made from some berry that grew on the meadowlands beyond the town and it sold a penny a cup to warm their stomachs, but not many were buying, not many had the wealth.

Tom stared ahead to the place where the line ended, beyond a bombed-out stone wall.

'They say she *smiles*,' said the boy.

'Aye, she does,' said Grigsby.

'They say she's made of oil and canvas.'

'True. And that's what makes me think she's not the original one. The original, now, I've heard, was painted on wood a long time ago.'

'They say she's four centuries old.'

'Maybe more. No one knows what year this is, to be sure.'

'It's 2061!'

'That's what they say, boy, yes. Liars. Could be 3000 or 5000 for all we know. Things were a fearful mess there for a while. All we got now is bits and pieces.'

They shuffled along the cold stones of the street.

'How much longer before we see her?' asked Tom, uneasily.

'Just a few more minutes. They got her set up with four brass poles and velvet rope, all fancy, to keep folks back. Now mind, no rocks, Tom; they don't allow rocks thrown at her.'

'Yes, sir.'

The sun rose higher in the heavens, bringing heat which made the men shed their grimy coats and greasy hats.

'Why're we all here in line?' asked Tom, at last. 'Why're we all here to spit?'

Grigsby did not glance down at him, but judged the sun. 'Well, Tom, there's lots of reasons.' He reached absently for a pocket that was long gone, for a cigarette that wasn't there. Tom had seen the gesture a million times. 'Tom, it has to do with hate. Hate for everything in the Past. I ask you, Tom, how did we get in such a state, cities all junk, roads like jig-saws from bombs, and half the cornfields glowing with radioactivity at night? Ain't that a lousy stew, I ask you?'

'Yes, sir, I guess so.'

'It's this way, Tom. You hate whatever it was that got you all knocked down and ruined. That's human nature. Unthinking, maybe, but human nature anyway.'

'There's hardly nobody or nothing we don't hate,' said Tom.

'Right! The whole blooming caboodle of them people in the Past who run the world. So here we are on a Thursday morning with our guts plastered to our spines, cold, live in caves and such, don't smoke, don't drink, don't nothing except have our festivals, Tom, our festivals.'

And Tom thought of the festivals in the past few years.

The year they tore up all the books in the square and burned them and everyone was drunk and laughing. And the festival of science a month ago when they dragged in the last motor-car and picked lots and each lucky man who won was allowed one smash of a sledge-hammer at the car.

'Do I remember *that*, Tom? Do I *remember*? Why, I got to smash the front window, the window, you hear? My God, it made a lovely sound! *Crash!*'

Tom could hear the glass falling in glittering heaps.

'And Bill Henderson, he got to bash the engine. Oh, he did a smart job of it, with great efficiency. *Wham!*'

But the best of all, recalled Grigsby, there was the time they smashed a factory that was still trying to turn out aeroplanes.

'Lord, did we feel good blowing it up!' said Grigsby. 'And then we found that newspaper plant and the munitions depot and exploded them together. Do you understand, Tom?'

Tom puzzled over it. 'I guess.'

It was high noon. Now the odours of the ruined city stank on the hot air and things crawled among the tumbled buildings.

'Won't it ever come back, mister?'

'What, civilisation? Nobody wants it. Not me!'

'I could stand a bit of it,' said the man behind another man. 'There were a few spots of beauty in it.'

'Don't worry your heads,' shouted Grigsby. 'There's no room for that, either.'

'Ah,' said the man behind the man. 'Someone'll come along some day with imagination and patch it up. Mark my words. Someone with a heart.'

'No,' said Grigsby.

'I say yes. Someone with a soul for pretty things. Might give us back a kind of *limited* sort of civilisation, the kind we could live in in peace.'

'First thing you know there's war!'

'But maybe next time it'd be different.'

At last they stood in the main square. A man on horseback was riding from the distance into the town. He had a piece of paper in his hand. In the centre of the square was the roped-off area. Tom, Grigsby, and the others were collecting their spittle and moving forward – moving forward prepared and ready, eyes wide. Tom felt his heart beating very strongly and excitedly, and the earth was hot under his bare feet.

'Here we go, Tom, let fly!'

Four policemen stood at the corners of the roped area, four men with bits of yellow twine on their wrists to show their authority over other men. They were there to prevent rocks being hurled.

'This way,' said Grigsby at the last moment, 'everyone feels he's had his chance at her, you see, Tom? Go on, now!'

Tom stood before the painting and looked at it for a long time.

'Tom, spit!'

His mouth was dry.

'Get on, Tom! Move!'

'But,' said Tom, slowly, 'she's beautiful!'

'Here, I'll spit for you!' Grigsby spat and the missile flew in the sunlight. The woman in the portrait smiled serenely, secretly at Tom, and he looked back at her, his heart beating, a kind of music in his ears.

'She's beautiful,' he said.

The line fell silent. One moment they were berating Tom for not moving forward, now they were turning to the man on horseback.

'What do they call it, sir?' asked Tom, quietly.

'The picture? *Mona Lisa*, Tom, I think. Yes, the *Mona Lisa*.'

'I have an announcement,' said the man on horseback. 'The authorities have decreed that as of high noon today the portrait in the square is to be given over into the hands of the populace there, so they may participate in the destruction of –'

Tom hadn't even time to scream before the crowd bore him, shouting and pummelling about, stampeding towards the portrait. There was a sharp ripping sound. The police ran to escape. The crowd was in full cry, their hands like so many hungry birds pecking away at the portrait. Tom felt himself thrust almost through the broken thing. Reaching out in blind imitation of the others, he snatched a scrap of oily canvas, yanked, felt the canvas give, then fell, was kicked, sent rolling to the outer rim of the mob. Bloody, his clothing torn, he watched old women chew pieces of canvas, men break the frame, kick the ragged cloth, and rip it into confetti.

Only Tom stood apart, silent in the moving square. he looked down at his hand. It clutched the piece of canvas close to his chest, hidden.

'Hey there, Tom!' called Grigsby.

Without a word, sobbing, Tom ran. He ran out and down the bomb-pitted road, into a field, across a shallow stream, not looking back, his hand clenched tightly, tucked under his coat.

At sunset he reached the small village and passed on through. By nine o'clock he came to the ruined farm dwelling. Around the back, in the half-silo, in the part that still remained upright, tented over,he heard the sounds of sleeping, the family – his mother, father, and brother. He slipped quickly, silently, through the small door and lay down panting.

'Tom?' called his mother in the dark.

'Yes.'

'Where've you been?' snapped his father. 'I'll beat you in the morning.'

Someone kicked him. His brother, who had been left behind to work their little patch of ground.

'Go to sleep,' cried his mother, faintly.

Another kick.

Tom lay getting his breath. All was quiet. His hand was pushed to his chest, tight, tight. He lay for half an hour this way, eyes closed.

Then he felt something, and it was a cold white light. The moon rose very high and the little square of light moved in the silo and crept slowly over Tom's body. Then, and only then, did his hand relax. Slowly, carefully, listening to those who slept about him, Tom drew his hand forth. He hesitated, sucked in his breath, and then, waiting, opened his hand and uncrumpled the tiny fragment of painted canvas.

All the world asleep in the moonlight.

And there on his hand was the Smile.

He looked at it in the white illumination from the midnight sky. And he thought, over and over to himself, quietly, *the Smile, the lovely Smile.*

An hour later he could still see it, even after he had folded it carefully and hidden it. He shut his eyes and the Smile was there in the darkness. And it was still there, warm and gentle, when he went to sleep and the world was silent and the moon sailed up and then down the cold sky towards morning.

*Ray Bradbury*

# 29

# A Teaching Machine

The sign in the window said: SCHOOL-TEACHER FOR SALE, DIRT CHEAP; and, in small letters: can cook, sew and is handy round the house.

She made Danby think of desks and erasers; of books and dreams and laughter. The proprietor of the little second-hand store had adorned her with a gay-coloured dress and had slipped little red sandals on her feet, and she stood in her upright case in the window like a life-size doll waiting for someone to bring her to life.

Danby tried to move on down the street to the parking lot where he kept his Baby Buick. Laura probably had his supper all dialled and waiting on the table for him and she would be furious if he was late. He'd passed the store a thousand times on his way from the parking lot to his office and on his way from the office to the parking lot, but this was the first time he'd ever stopped and looked in the window.

But wasn't  this the first time the window had ever contained something he'd wanted?

Danby tried to face the question. Did he *want* a school-teacher? Well hardly. But Laura certainly needed someone to help her with the housework and they couldn't afford an automatic maid, and Billy certainly could stand some extra-TV tutoring, with the box-top tests coming up, and, and . . .

Antiques of every description were scattered about the interior of the store. The proprietor was a little old man with bushy white hair and gingerbread eyes. He looked like an antique himself.

He beamed at Danby's question. 'You like her, sir?'

'How much is she?' Danby repeated.

'Forty-nine ninety-five, plus five dollars for the case.'

Danby could hardly believe it. With school-teachers so rare, you'd think the price would go up, not down. And yet, less than a year ago, when he'd been thinking of buying a re-built third grade teacher to help Billy with his TV schoolwork, the lowest priced one he could find had run well over a hundred dollars. He would have bought her even at that, though, if Laura hadn't talked him out of it. Laura had never gone to realschool and didn't understand.

But forty-nine ninety-five! And she could cook and sew too! Surely Laura wouldn't try to talk him out of buying this one—

She definitely wouldn't if he didn't give her the chance.

'Is – is she in good condition?'

The proprietor's face grew pained. 'She's been completely overhauled, sir. Brand new batteries, and motors. Her tapes are good for another ten years yet, and her memory banks will probably last for ever. Here. I'll bring her in and show you.'

The case was mounted on castors, but it was awkward to handle. Danby helped the old man push it out of the window and into the store. They stood by the door where the light was brightest.

The old man stepped back admiringly. 'Maybe I'm old-fashioned,' he said, 'but I say that teleteachers will never compare to the real thing. You went to realschool, didn't you, sir?'

Danby nodded.

'I thought so. Funny the way you can always tell.'

'Turn her on, please,' Danby said.

The activator was a tiny button, hidden behind the left ear lobe. The proprietor fumbled for a moment before he found it. Then there was a little click!, followed by a soft, almost inaudible purring sound. Presently, colour crept into the cheeks, the breast began to rise and fall; blue eyes opened –

'Make her say something.'

'She responds to almost everything, sir,' the old man said. 'Words, scenes, situations ... if you decide to take her and aren't satisfied, bring her back and I'll be glad to refund the money.' He faced the case. 'What is your name?' he asked.

'Miss Jones.' Her voice was a September wind.

'Your occupation?'

'Specifically, I'm a fourth grade teacher, sir, but I can substitute for first, second, third, fifth, sixth, seven and eighth grades, and I'm well grounded in the humanities. Also I'm proficient in household chores, am a qualified cook, and can perform simple tasks, such as sewing on buttons, darning socks, and repairing rips and tears in clothing.'

'They put a lot of extras in the later models,' the old man said in an aside to Danby. 'When they finally realised that tele-education was here to stay, they started doing everything they could to beat the cereal companies. But it didn't do any good.' Then: 'Step outside your case, Miss Jones. Show us how nice you walk.'

She walked once around the drab room, her little red sandals twinkling over the dusty floor, her dress a gay little rainfall of colour. Then she returned and stood waiting by the door.

Danby hesitated for a moment. 'All right,' he said finally. 'Put her back in her case. I'll take her.' *Robert Young*

109

# 30

# There Will Come Soft Rains

In the living room the voice-clock sang, *Tick-tock, seven o'clock, time to get up, time to get up, seven o'clock!* as if it were afraid that nobody would. The morning house lay empty. The clock ticked on, repeating and repeating its sounds into the emptiness. *Seven-nine, breakfast time, seven-nine!*

In the kitchen the breakfast stove gave a hissing sigh and ejected from its warm interior eight pieces of perfectly browned toast, eight eggs sunnyside up, sixteen slices of bacon, two coffees, and two cool glasses of milk.

'Today is August 4, 2026,' said a second voice from the kitchen ceiling, 'in the city of Allendale, California.' It repeated the date three times for memory's sake. 'Today is Mr Featherstone's birthday. Today is the anniversary of Tilita's marriage. Insurance is payable, as are the water, gas, and light bills.'

Somewhere in the walls, relays clicked, memory tapes glided under electric eyes.

*Eight-one, tick-tock, eight-one o'clock, off to school, off to work, run, run, eight-one!* But no doors slammed, no carpets took the soft tread of rubber heels. It was raining outside. The weather box on the front door sang quietly: 'Rain, rain, go away; rubbers, raincoats for today ...' And the rain tapped on the empty house, echoing.

Outside, the garage chimed and lifted its door to reveal the waiting car. After a long wait the door swung down again.

At eight-thirty the eggs were shrivelled and the toast was like stone. An aluminium wedge scraped them into the sink, where hot water whirled them down a metal throat which digested and flushed them away to the distant sea. The dirty dishes were dropped into a hot washer and emerged twinkling dry.

*Nine-fifteen,* sang the clock, *time to clean.*

Out of warrens in the wall, tiny robot mice darted. The rooms were acrawl with the small cleaning animals, all rubber and metal. They thudded against chairs, whirling their moustached runners, kneading the rug nap, sucking gently at hidden dust. Then, like mysterious invaders, they popped into their burrows. Their pink electric eyes faded. The house was clean.

*Ten o'clock.* The sun came out from behind the rain. The house stood alone in a city of rubble and ashes. This was the one house left standing. At night the ruined city gave off a radioactive glow which could be seen for miles.

*Ten-fifteen.* The garden sprinklers whirled up in golden founts, filling the soft morning air with scatterings of brightness. The water pelted windowpanes, running down the charred west side where the house had been burned evenly free of its white paint. The entire west face of the house was black, save for five places. Here the silhouette in paint of a man mowing a lawn. Here, as in a photograph, a woman bent to pick flowers. Still farther over, their images burned on wood in one titanic instant, a small boy, hands flung into the air; higher up, the image of a thrown ball, and opposite him a girl, hands raised to catch a ball which never came down.

The five spots of paint – the man, the woman, the children, the ball – remained. The rest was a thin charcoaled layer.

The gentle sprinkler rain filled the garden with falling light.

Until this day, how well the house had kept its peace. How carefully it had inquired, 'Who goes there? What's the password?' and, getting no answer from lonely foxes and whining cats, it had shut up its windows and drawn shades in an old-maidenly preoccupation with self-protection which bordered on a mechanical paranoia.

It quivered at each sound, the house did. If a sparrow brushed a window, the shade snapped up. The bird, startled, flew off! No, not even a bird must touch the house!

The house was an altar with ten thousand attendants, big, small, servicing, attending, in choirs. But the gods had gone away, and the ritual of the religion continued senselessly, uselessly.

*Twelve noon.*

A dog whined, shivering, on the front porch.

The front door recognized the dog voice and opened. The dog, once huge and fleshy, but now gone to bone and covered with sores, moved in and through the house, tracking mud. Behind it whirred angry mice, angry at having to pick up mud, angry at inconvenience.

For not a leaf fragment blew under the door but what the wall panels flipped open and the copper scrap rats flashed swiftly out. The offending dust, hair, or paper, seized in miniature steel jaws, was raced back to the burrows. There, down tubes which fed into the cellar, it was dropped into the sighing vent of an incinerator which sat like evil Baal in a dark corner.

The dog ran upstairs, hysterically yelping to each door, at last realizing, as the house realized, that only silence was here.

It sniffed the air and scratched the kitchen door. Behind the door, the stove was making pancakes which filled the house with a rich baked odour and the scent of maple syrup.

The dog frothed at the mouth, lying at the door, sniffing, its eyes turned to fire. It ran wildly in circles, biting at its tail, spun in a frenzy, and died. It lay in the parlour for an hour.

*Two o'clock*, sang a voice.

Delicately sensing decay at last, the regiments of mice hummed out as softly as blown grey leaves in an electrical wind.

*Two-fifteen.*

The dog was gone.

In the cellar, the incinerator glowed suddenly and a whirl of sparks leaped up the chimney.

*Two thirty-five.*

Bridge tables sprouted from patio walls. Playing cards fluttered onto pads in a shower of pips. Martinis manifested on an oaken bench with egg-salad sandwiches. Music played.

But the tables were silent and the cards untouched.

At four o'clock the tables folded like great butterflies back through the panelled walls.

*Four-thirty.*

The nursery walls glowed.

Animals took shape: yellow giraffes, blue lions, pink antelopes, lilac panthers cavorting in crystal substance. The walls were glass. They looked out upon colour and fantasy. Hidden films clocked through well-oiled sprockets, and the walls lived. The nursery floor was woven to resemble a crisp, cereal meadow. Over this ran aluminium roaches and iron crickets, and in the hot still air butterflies of delicate red tissue wavered among the sharp aromas of animal spoors! There was the sound like a great matted yellow hive of bees within a dark bellows, the lazy bumble of a purring lion. And there was the patter of okapi feet and the murmur of a fresh jungle rain, like other hoofs, falling upon the summer-starched grass. Now the walls dissolved into distances of parched weed, mile on mile, and warm endless sky. The animals drew away into thorn brakes and water holes.

It was the children's hour.

*Five o'clock.* The bath filled with clear hot water.

*Six, seven, eight o'clock.* The dinner dishes manipulated like magic tricks, and in the study a *click.* In the metal stand opposite the hearth where a fire now blazed up warmly, a cigar popped out, half an inch of soft grey ash on it, smoking, waiting.

*Nine o'clock.* The beds warmed their hidden circuits, for nights were cool here.

*Nine-five.* A voice spoke from the study ceiling:

'Mrs McClellan, which poem would you like this evening?'

The house was silent.

The voice said at last, 'Since you express no preference, I shall select a poem at random.' Quiet music rose to back the voice. 'Sara Teasdale. As I recall, your favourite . . .

*There will come soft rains and the smell of the ground,*
*And swallows circling with their shimmering sound;*

*And frogs in the pools singing at night,*
*And wild plum trees in tremulous white;*

*Robins will wear their feathery fire,*
*Whistling their whims on a low fence-wire;*

*And not one will know of the war, not one*
*Will care at last when it is done.*

*Not one would mind, neither bird nor tree,*
*If mankind perished utterly;*

*And Spring herself, when she woke at dawn*
*Would scarcely know that we were gone.'*

The fire burned on the stone hearth and the cigar fell away into a mound of quiet ash on its tray. The empty chairs faced each other between the silent walls, and the music played.

At ten o'clock the house began to die.

The wind blew. A falling tree bough crashed through the kitchen window. Cleaning solvent, bottled, shattered over the stove. The room was ablaze in an instant!

'Fire!' screamed a voice. The house lights flashed, water pumps shot water from the ceiling. But the solvent spread on the linoleum, licking, eating, under the kitchen door, while the voices took it up in chorus: 'Fire, fire, fire!'

The house tried to save itself. Doors sprang tightly shut, but the windows were broken by the heat and the wind blew and sucked upon the fire.

The house gave ground as the fire in ten billion angry sparks moved with flaming ease from room to room and then up the stairs. While scurrying water rats squeaked from the walls, pistolled their water, and ran for more. And the wall sprays let down showers of mechanical rain.

But too late. Somewhere, sighing, a pump shrugged to a stop. The quenching rain ceased. The reserve water supply which had filled baths and washed dishes for many quiet days was gone.

The fire crackled up the stairs. It fed upon Picassos and Matisses in the upper halls, like delicacies, baking off the oily flesh, tenderly crisping the canvases into black shavings.

Now the fire lay in beds, stood in windows, changed the colours of drapes!

And then, reinforcements.

From attic trapdoors, blind robot faces peered down with faucet mouths gushing green chemical.

The fire backed off, as even an elephant must at the sight of a dead snake. Now there were twenty snakes whipping over the floor, killing the fire with a clear cold venom of green froth.

But the fire was clever. It had sent flame outside the house, up through the attic to the pumps there. An explosion! The attic brain which directed the pumps was shattered into bronze shrapnel on the beams.

The fire rushed back into every closet and felt of the clothes hung there.

The house shuddered, oak bone on bone, its bared skeleton cringing from the heat, its wire, its nerves revealed as if a surgeon had torn the skin off to let the red veins and capillaries quiver in the scalded air. Help, help! Fire! Run, run! Heat snapped mirrors like the first brittle winter ice. And the voices wailed, Fire, fire, run, run, like a tragic nursery rhyme, a dozen voices, high, low, like children dying in a forest, alone, alone. And the voices fading as the wires popped their sheathings like hot chestnuts. One, two, three, four, five voices died.

In the nursery the jungle burned. Blue lions roared, purple giraffes bounded off. The panthers ran in circles, changing colour, and ten million animals, running before the fire, vanished off towards a distant streaming river . . .

Ten more voices died. In the last instant under the fire avalanche, other choruses, oblivious, could be heard announcing the time, playing music, cutting the lawn by remote-control mower, or setting an umbrella frantically out and in, the slamming and opening front door, a thousand things happening, like a clock shop when each clock strikes the hour insanely before or after the other, a scene of maniac confusion, yet unity; singing, screaming, a few last cleaning mice darting bravely out to carry the horrid ashes away! And one voice, with sublime disregard for the situation, read poetry aloud in the fiery study, until all the film spools burned, until all the wires withered and the circuits cracked.

The fire burst the house and let it slam flat down, puffing out skirts of spark and smoke.

In the kitchen, an instant before the rain of fire and timber, the stove could be seen making breakfasts at a psychopathic rate, ten dozen eggs, six loaves of toast, twenty dozen bacon strips, which, eaten by fire, started the stove working again, hysterically hissing!

The crash. The attic smashing into kitchen and parlour. The parlour into cellar, cellar into sub-cellar. Deep freeze, armchair, film tapes, circuits, beds, and all like skeletons thrown in a cluttered mound deep under.

Smoke and silence. A great quantity of smoke.

Dawn showed faintly in the east. Among the ruins, one wall stood alone. Within the wall, a last voice said, over and over again and again, even as the sun rose to shine upon the heaped rubble and steam:

'Today is August 5, 2026, today is August 5, 2026, today is . . .'

*Ray Bradbury*

# 31

# At Lunchtime
# A Story of Love

When the busstopped suddenly to avoid
damaging a mother and child in the road, the
younglady in the greenhat sitting opposite
was thrown across me, and not being one to
miss an opportunity i started to makelove
with all my body.

At first she resisted saying that it
was tooearly in the morning and toosoon
after breakfast and that anyway she found
me repulsive. But when i explained that
this being a nuclearage, the world was going
to end at lunchtime, she tookoff her
greenhat, put her busticket in her pocket
and joined in the exercise.

The buspeople, and therewere many of
them, were shockedandsurprised and amused-
andannoyed, but when the word got around
that the world was coming to an end at lunchtime, they put their pride in their pockets
with their bustickets and madelove one with
the other. And even the busconductor, being
over, climbed into the cab and struck up
some sort of relationship with the driver.

Thatnight, on the bus coming home,
wewere all alittle embarrassed, especially me
and the younglady in the greenhat, and we
all started to say in different ways howhasty
and foolish we had been. Butthen, always
having been a bitofalad, i stood up and
said it was a pity that the world didn't nearly
end every lunchtime and that we could always
pretend. And then it happened . . .

Quick asa crash we all changed partners
and soon the bus was aquiver with white
mothballbodies doing naughty things.

And the next day
And everyday
In everybus
In everystreet
In everytown
In everycountry

people pretended that the world was coming
to an end at lunchtime. It still hasn't.
Although in a way it has.

Roger McGough

# 32

# Icarus Allsorts

'A meteorite is reported to have landed
in New England. No damage is said . . .'

A littlebit of heaven fell
From out the sky one day
It landed in the ocean
Not so very far away
The General at the radar screen
Rubbed his hands with glee
And grinning pressed the button
That started World War Three.

From every corner of the earth
Bombs began to fly
There were even missile jams
No traffic lights in the sky
In the times it takes to blow your nose
The people fell, the mushrooms rose

'House!' cried the fatlady
As the bingohall moved to various parts
of the town

'Raus!' cried the German butcher
as his shop came tumbling down

Philip was in the countinghouse
Counting out his money
The Queen was in the parlour
Eating bread and honey
When through the window
Flew a bomb
And made them go all funny

In the time it takes to draw a breath
Or eat a toadstool, instant death.

The rich
Huddled outside the doors of their fallout shelters
Like drunken carolsingers

The poor
Clutching shattered televisions
And last week's edition of T.V. Times
(but the very last)

Civil defence volunteers
Withtheir tin hats in one hand
And their heads in the other

CND supporters
Their ban the bomb badges beginning to rust
Have scrawled 'I told you so' in the dust.

A littlebit of heaven fell
From out the sky one day
It landed in Vermont
North-Eastern U.S.A.
The general at the radar screen
He should have got the sack
But that wouldn't bring
Three thousand million, seven hundred,
    and sixty-eight people back,
Would it?

Roger McGough

# 33

# Noah's Arc

In my fallout shelter I have enough food
For at least three months. Some books,
Scrabble, and games for the children.
Calor gas and candles. Comfortable beds
And a chemical toilet. Under lock and key
The tools necessary for a life after death.
I have carried out my instructions to the letter.

Most evenings I'm down here. Checking the stores,
Our suits, breathing apparatus. Cleaning
And polishing. My wife, bless her,
Thinks I'm obsessive – like other men
About cars or football. But deep down
She understands. I have no hobbies.
My sole interest is survival.

Every few weeks we have what I call D.D.,
Or Disaster Drill. At the sound of the alarm
We each go about our separate duties:
Disconnecting services, switching off the mains,
Filling the casks with fresh water, etc.
Mine is to oversee everything before finally
Shooting the dog. (This I mime in private.)

At first, the young ones enjoyed the days
And nights spent below. It was an adventure.
But now they're at a difficult age
And regard extinction as the boring concern
Of grown-ups. Like divorce and accountancy.
But I am firm. Daddy knows best
And one fine day they'll grow to thank me.

Beneath my bunk I keep an Armalite rifle
Loaded and ready to use one fine day
When panicking neighbours and so-called friends
Try to clamber aboard. The ones who scoff,
Who ignore the signs. I have my orders,
There will be no stowaways. No gatecrashers
At my party. A party starting soon.

And the sooner the better. Like a grounded
Astronaut I grow daily more impatient.
Am on tenterhooks. Each night
I ask the Lord to get on with it.
I fear sometimes He has forsaken us,
We His favourite children. Meek, drilled,
And ready to inherit an earth, newly-cleansed.

I scan the headlines, watch the screen.
A doctor thrilling at each fresh tumour:
The latest invasion, a breakdown of talks.
I pray for malignancy. The self-induced
Sickness for which there is only one cure:
Radium treatment. The final absolution.
That part of full circle we have yet to come.

*Roger McGough*